J. Terry Johnson

A Glorious Church

TRACING RESTORATION MOVEMENTS
THROUGH THE CENTURIES

RESEARCH AND COLLABORATIVE ASSISTANCE BY
Greg Neill

Editing by Kylie Lyons
Cover and Interior Design by Kandi Evans

Published by Clarity Publications, Oklahoma City, Oklahoma

ISBN:978-0-9884051-3-4
1. Religion: Christianity
2. Church History

08.20.15

Acknowledgments

I enjoy reading history. My pleasure is not in the detail, but in the broad sweeping strokes that paint an overview of how things have come about to be the way they are. The present can always be interpreted in some measure by the past.

Talented teachers of secondary social studies classes contributed to my interest in history. Some history and political science professors at Oklahoma Christian University and Southern Methodist University did the same. I am especially grateful for Dr. Joseph F. Jones, who taught my undergraduate classes in Church History and my study of the Protestant Reformation.

Greg Neill, a gospel preacher and a brilliant student of God's word, has made a sizeable contribution to the development of *A Glorious Church*. He has supplied me with fresh material that I would have overlooked without his counsel. Greg is also responsible for compiling the bibliography and drafting the discussion questions designed to help those who choose to use this book as a study guide for teaching a class.

I am again grateful to my editor, Kylie Lyons and graphic designer, Kandi Evans. This is the seventh book on which they have collaborated with me, and I have always found them to be the consummate professionals.

My gratitude is also extended to a few cherished friends who read my manuscript in its formative stage, and offered constructive suggestions for improving the book's content and accuracy. Notably, Lynn McMillon and Guy Ross of Oklahoma City, Oklahoma, along with Hardeman Nichols and Gary Hill of Dallas, Texas, comprised my trusted team of advisors. The reader has no way of knowing the vital contribution these men made to the storyline, but I am aware of their favorable influence in virtually every chapter.

Finally, I am delighted to work once again with Clarity Publications. Clarity published one of my first books, *Fairways and Green Pastures*, and I appreciate the working relationship we have enjoyed over the years.

Dedication

Many teachers have influenced the direction of my life, and I am grateful to each of them. Some grounded me in general studies that were part of the curricula of the Springfield, Missouri, Public Schools. A distinguished faculty of professors at Southern Methodist University's School of Law capped my formal education with challenging courses in jurisprudence.

Between those two learning experiences, however, I encountered a talented undergraduate faculty of unheralded superstars at Oklahoma Christian College in Oklahoma City. These professors stimulated my mind while stirring the juices of my soul. They introduced me to new thoughts, to provocative authors and titles, and to the fascinating subject of "church history."

A Glorious Church is dedicated to the memory of professors Hugo McCord, Joseph F. Jones, William E. Jones, James O. Baird, and Raymond C. Kelcy, who taught my Bible classes at Oklahoma Christian during the 1960s. Today, I stand on their shoulders.

Table of Contents

Introduction

While attending the National Prayer Breakfast in Washington, D.C., a few years ago, I was privileged to hear former Secretary of State Condoleezza Rice share a few thoughts regarding the importance of her own spiritual journey, especially the encouragement she had always received from her family. The child of two educators—a father who was a high school teacher, guidance counselor, and an ordained Presbyterian minister; a mother who taught school and was the organist at her local church—Rice was a child prodigy. She began taking piano lessons when she was three years old and performed in her first public recital one year later.

At the prayer breakfast, Secretary Rice recounted an incident in which she was approached in the supermarket by a stranger who asked if she would be willing to play the piano at his small church in Palo Alto, California. After mulling over the request for a few days, she cautiously accepted his invitation. For several weeks Ms. Rice faithfully played hymns at the Sunday morning worship services, trying her best to keep up with the pastor, who, without warning, had a habit of breaking into song to illustrate a key point in his lesson. Because she never knew which key he might use, it always took her a moment or two to get in harmony with the pastor's musical outbursts. Unsure as to whether she was properly suited for this new role, Ms. Rice sought advice from her mother and was reassured with these words: "Honey, just play in the *key of C* and he'll always come back to you."

As I examine the material that has prompted me to write this book, I find myself searching for Middle C. Who among us has a perfect understanding of the New Testament church as it originally existed in the mind of God? How can anyone accurately assess the damage that has been done by church leaders who have bound human traditions on ardent believers over hundreds of years? By what process can any generation faithfully restore the church to its apostolic roots? Forget Middle C—where can we locate a suitable keyboard?

Of this I am certain: I am a *restorer*. I believe it is of great importance for Christians to keep the "bride of Christ" as uncontaminated today as it was on that Pentecostal Sunday when Peter spoke to the multitude that had gathered in Jerusalem. The church was in its infancy, as innocent and pure as a newborn baby taking his first breath. Over the passing of centuries, that purity has been besmirched by the sinful will of its leaders who have substituted their own partialities for governing the church in place of the inspired words of those apostolic leaders who were present when the church was founded.

Not everyone is an advocate for restoration theology. Some who once embraced this approach to biblical interpretation have given up in favor of a more culturally inspired hermeneutic. What can I say? I may err in my interpretation of the Scripture, but I prefer to find my basis for church doctrine and practices in the sacred words and traditions of the apostles rather than follow the whims of modern culture.

If I were a member of the United States Supreme Court, I would be styled by the Washington pundits as a *strict constructionist*. Justices of this stripe adhere closely to the words and intent of the "founding fathers" who framed the Constitution. Their honorable colleagues who think otherwise are known as *activists*. They find it perfectly permissible to interpret laws in light of societal whims, often resulting in new law being created by their own judicial pronouncements. What amazes me is that justices who differ so greatly in their approaches to legal interpretation still treat each other with respect. I wish it were more that way with those of us who differ in the interpretation of Scripture. Christians should be able to take strong positions for what they believe without demeaning one another or wishing their adversaries an eternal home in hell.

A Glorious Church is not intended to be a definitive work recounting centuries of church history, nor is it meant to resolve the many theological differences that have made it difficult for Christians to work together in the past. It is a cursory review of the events that have shaped the church from its inception until modern time, noting those innovations that have pulled it away from its moorings and highlighting key individuals who have tried to restore the body to its original doctrine and practices. The appeal is to reinstate both *form* and *spirit* of the New Testament church, drawing upon apostolic teachings, time-honored practices dating from the first century, and a measure of common sense.

My audience is not the many scholars who have read the writings of Ante-Nicene fathers or have written learned articles on the minutiae of church history. Rather, I'm hoping to reach a lesser-informed audience of those who may not see themselves as people who enjoy reading any form of ecclesiastical history but do have a curiosity about the evolution of the church over the past two thousand years. *A Glorious Church* is what some might call *church history lite*: more about the big picture, less about the detail.

May God bless all who study his word, and may the reading of *A Glorious Church* bring fresh perspective to the beauty of God's perfect design for the church—the body and the bride of Jesus Christ.

1

A Glorious Church:

Holy and without Blemish
A.D. 29 – 100

By the time we reach adulthood, most of us have attended our share of weddings. It has been my privilege to officiate a few of those blessed events. Some have been formal—tediously planned and orchestrated down to the last piece of rice thrown at the escaping wedding party. One service was so informal that none of us stood during the entire event. The bride, the groom, two witnesses, and I sat in living room chairs, working our way through the vows, the ring exchange, and the obligatory kiss to seal the promises. From what I could tell, it was legal and went exactly as the bride had requested.

I may never forget the summer day in Colorado when my nephew and his bride exchanged their vows. The church was so hot that guests were offered chilled bottles of water and battery-operated fans as they entered the un-air-conditioned auditorium. While in the middle of assisting the bride with her vow, I saw something alarming from the corner of my eye. The best man had keeled over like a piece of timber. A doctor, summoned from the audience, tended to the young man, and we all lived to tell about the harrowing event. The collapse, caught on video, ran for several years on a syndicated television show that featured wacky wedding scenes.

Then there was the wedding in Oklahoma that had to be put on pause for a few minutes until the groom could compose himself. Upon seeing his bride walk down the aisle, arm in arm with her father, the groom broke into sniffles. I didn't think too much of it until his tearful whimpers turned into audible sobs that kept him from participating in the ritual. After a brief pause and some back patting from the groomsmen, we proceeded with the formalities.

A beautiful bride is a spectacular attraction. She radiates loveliness, purity, and worth that is "far above rubies" (Prov. 31:10). We should not be surprised that the apostle Paul exhorted husbands to

> *"...love your wives just as Christ also loved the church and gave himself for her, that he might sanctify and cleanse her with the washing of water by the word, that he might present her to himself a glorious church, not having spot or wrinkle or any such thing, but that she should be holy and without blemish." (Eph. 5:25-27)*

I grasp the point that the perfection of the church is a result of the sacrifice that Christ has made on its behalf. If it were not for our savior's death on the cross, it would be impossible to describe the church as being "without blemish." Nonetheless, I am impressed when reading this passage that God's original intent was for the bride of Christ to be "a glorious church, not having spot or wrinkle." As we contemplate what reputation the church has today, we cannot be happy with any shame or degradation that *we* may have brought to the bride of Christ. To the extent that it is within our power, we need to give ourselves to the work of restoring the glory and the purity of the Lord's church as it existed in its inception.

Restoration is not a novel concept that belongs exclusively to our own generation. The process has always been seen as a way for

God's people to identify foreign practices and erroneous doctrines, either eliminating or amending them, and drawing the righteous closer to God's heart. Many excellent examples of restoration can be found in the Old Testament.

Hezekiah, who reigned as king of Judah for twenty-nine years, was a ruler who held fast to the Lord (2 Kings 18 ff.). He tore down altars and shrines that were used by his people to worship pagan gods. He even destroyed the bronze serpent that Moses had made in the wilderness because it, too, had become an object of worship, the children of Israel offering incense to it as if it were a god. God rewarded Hezekiah's faithfulness, giving him victory over the Assyrian king Sennacherib and eventually extending Hezekiah's life by fifteen years.

Following Hezekiah's reign, however, the kings of Judah again abandoned the ways of the Lord, did evil deeds, and adopted idolatrous forms of worship. The kingdom desperately needed reform. Josiah, the boy who became king when he was eight years old, brought restoration to his people. He is hailed in 2 Kings 22 as having done "what was right in the sight of the Lord, and walked in all the ways of his father David; he did not turn aside to the right hand or to the left" (2 Ki. 22:2).

Moreover, Josiah, after learning about the high priest's discovery of the Book of the Law, God's word that had been neglected for years, spent the latter part of his thirty-one-year reign restoring what had been lost. He and the people made a covenant with God to follow more explicitly the teaching of his word. Idolatrous practices and shrines were removed, and observance of the Passover was reinstated (2 Kings 22, 23). In his generation, Josiah was a restorer, and that became his legacy.

Now transfer the experiences of Hezekiah and Josiah to our own times. How would God-fearing Christians begin the process of restoring the twenty-first century church to something akin to what it was two thousand years ago? Where on the restoration game board is the square marked "GO?"

In recent years, the search has led many church leaders to seek answers from high-profile preachers who have enjoyed uncommon success in building "mega churches." They have made the trek to Chicago, where Bill Hybels has led a dynamic body known as Willow Creek Community Church. Others have traveled to the West Coast, examining the Saddleback Church, where Rick Warren's leadership and highly popular books have made an enormous impact for Christian discipleship. Caravans have streamed their way to Houston to hear Joel Osteen preach at Lakewood Church, where thousands of souls can be found worshipping each Sunday in an arena that was the former home of the National Basketball Association's Houston Rockets.

What these three organizations have in common is a fellowship that has enjoyed exceptional success in attracting the masses, dynamic preachers who deliver relevant sermons, and a host of ministry opportunities that beckon their members to get involved. If size and vitality were the only criteria, these three churches might be a good place to begin restoring the New Testament church. As we shall see, however, size and vitality hardly scratch the surface. When restoration is the objective, much more is required.

An even more likely place to begin a restoration makeover is to examine the churches that are mentioned in the New Testament. After all, these congregations were begun by some of the apostles and others that accompanied them on their missionary journeys. Surely we can learn what we need to know by looking at the organization, mission, and work of the church in such places as Jerusalem, Corinth, Thessalonica, and Philippi.

Let's make one of them our model and work from that blueprint to restore the contemporary church to what its first-century counterpart appeared to be.

We could only wish it were that easy.

Upon closer examination, it becomes evident that every congregation mentioned in the New Testament was either flawed by human error, or the Scripture does not reveal enough of the congregation's teachings and practices for it to serve as a reliable model. Some leaders in the Jerusalem church were trying to bind circumcision upon its members (Acts 15). The congregation in Corinth was beset with a host of problems, including divisiveness, immorality, abuses in the observation of the Lord's Supper, and the mishandling of miraculous spiritual gifts. Christians in Thessalonica had quit their work and become busybodies, sponging off of those who would support them. The church in Ephesus had lost its first love, the church in Laodicea had become lukewarm, and Paul's beloved brethren in Philippi had to contend with members who couldn't get along with one another. Which one of these congregations will make an ideal model for our restoration project? None of the above! They were all led by ordinary people who made their own mistakes and, in the process, led others astray.

First Century Congregations that Needed Some Measure of Restorative Correction

CHURCH LOCATION	SPIRITUAL ISSUE(S) NEEDING CORRECTION
JERUSALEM	Some members wanted to require Christians to be circumcised (Acts 15:1 ff.).
CORINTH	There were divisions among members; immoral behavior allowed to exist publicly; abusive observance of the Lord's Supper; misuse of spiritual gifts (1 Corinthians 1:10 ff., 5:1 ff., 11:17 ff., 12-14).
THESSALONICA	Members had quit working in anticipation of the second coming of Christ and were expecting their fellow Christians to support them (2 Thessalonians 3:6 ff.).
GALATIA	Judaizing teachers were teaching the gospel but adding additional commandments in order to be saved (Galatians 1:6 ff., 4:8 ff.).
EPHESUS	Members had lost their first love—the fervor of their faith (Revelation 2:1-4 ff.).
PHILIPPI	Members were quarreling with one another (Philippians 4:2-3).
COLOSSAE	Gnosticism and other false teachings were being advanced (Colossians 2, 3).
LAODICEA	Members had become self-sufficient with worldly goods and lukewarm in their zeal for the Lord (Revelation 3:14 ff.).

If we seek to restore the "glorious church," as Paul spoke of in his letter to the Ephesians, we need to refashion it in the likeness of its origin—the church as it existed in the mind of Jehovah God.

Impossible, you say. *How can any mortal know what was in the mind of Almighty God?*

Fair question. Here's my best answer.

Only by reading what the Holy Spirit instructed the apostles and other New Testament scribes to write to the early churches can we know God's divine will. Each exhortation, every rebuke, even the call for certain attitudes to change among the brethren can lead us to a better understanding of what the church was designed to be. The inspired commendation of those congregations' successes is equally important as the correction of their mistakes. Woven into the fabric of these passages, we can find the illusive model of what God had in mind for the church, the earthly representation of the kingdom of heaven.

As we examine the Scripture, three imperatives must be observed. The first is to handle the teachings from God's word with humility. Arrogance is never in order when trying to restore the church. Paul taught the early Christians in Philippi to "let this mind be in you which was also in Christ Jesus" (Phil. 2:5). Jesus was the personification of humility, having given up heaven to become a servant on earth and suffer a painful and shameful death on a Roman cross. He is the head of the body, the church. Our demeanor must replicate the same spirit as his.

Another mandate to be followed by those who would restore the New Testament church is to "love one another." How many times have we heard or read of Christians verbally beating the tar out of someone, behaving boorishly, all under the banner of "defending the truth?" Truth, as we shall see in later chapters, is critical to the restoration process. No one wants to spend energy trying to support a false model for the church. Yet our directive from the apostolic teaching is to "speak the truth in love" (Eph. 4:15). The theme is so critical to our restoring the "glorious church" that Jesus said, "By this all will know that you are my disciples, if you have love for one another" (John 13:35).

Finally, in our quest to find the church as it was conceived in the mind of God, all will come to naught if we treat Scripture as anything less than the word of God. Paul commended the church in Thessalonica for having received his apostolic directives "not as the word of men, but as it is in truth, the word of God, which also effectively works in you who believe" (1 Thessalonians 2:13). Scripture trumps culture. Scripture is more binding than human traditions. What we learn from reading the gospels and the epistles that were written to the first century churches will take us closer to the heart of God than the inventive thoughts of contemporary man.

Some discount the Scripture because it was written to a primary audience that lived more than two thousand years ago. *What is there to learn from an archaic epistle written by Paul to a first century church in Corinth?* That point has some relevance in our effort to define what is appropriate for the church in modern culture, but it does not mean we have nothing to learn from the inspired words of these apostles.

Consider this case in point: my wife loves to take golf lessons. I have too much pride to subject myself to this kind of humiliation. Nonetheless, I'm always picking up pointers from what the golf professionals are teaching my wife. I'm not the primary audience, but almost everything she has been taught is applicable to my golf game and me. So it is with the apostolic epistles. They may have been written specifically to churches that existed in the first century, but valuable lessons on how to worship, minister, and fellowship can also be learned by Christians living two millennia after the primary audience.

There is a homogenous thread that should run through all congregations of the New Testament church. Its members should be those who "walk in the light" (1 John 1:5-7). They should be "led by the Spirit of God" (Rom. 8:14). Their everyday lives should be edified by the words of Christ (Col. 3:16). Christians should make it a priority to assemble as a corporate body in order to exhort and encourage one another (Heb. 10:24-25). And, above all else, Christians should model the love for one another that Jesus described to his disciples. This is where the restoration of the New Testament church begins.

2

The Post-Apostolic Church

100 – 450

Looking through some rose-colored spectacles, I confess to having had a distorted view of the first century church and how it worshipped. As a young adult, I pictured early Christians meeting in neat little church buildings with handcrafted pews, a rough-hewn pulpit stand, and a table from which the Lord's Supper was served by several men, dressed in their best Sunday-go-to-meeting garments. A sign on the front door identified the place as the Church of Christ.

In my imagination, each congregation had its own elders, deacons, a local preacher, and a stable of good Bible school teachers. The order of worship was virtually the same as the practices at any of the congregations mentioned in the New Testament. Public prayers were led, early epistles from the apostles were circulated and read at the assembly, and someone with a lovely tenor voice led the congregation in hymns that were sung in four-part harmonies and without any instrumental accompaniment. Women were present but never spoke except to sing. The early church, in my naïve way of thinking, looked very similar to the congregation where I grew up in Springfield, Missouri.

Although there were important features that knit early congregations to one another, the homogeneity never extended as far as I mistakenly believed. Several congregations met in homes, some in the Roman catacombs, while others assembled in open areas large enough to accommodate a few hundred congregants. For the better part of two centuries, no buildings were constructed solely for the purpose of conducting church services, and no one had cornered the market on making signs that read "The Church of Christ Meets Here."

Music was more in the form of chants or traditional psalms that had been passed down from generation to generation in Jewish families. From historical documents that chronicle the early church, two elements of my unenlightened vision appear to have been fairly accurate: women were seen but rarely heard in the assembly, and music was sung acapella.

Some groups that met regularly for worship were large enough to have elders and deacons, and some were not. In addition to these local leaders, most of the apostles continued to provide guidance, speaking, and writing messages of encouragement and exhortation. These extraordinary leaders, with the exception of Mathias, were selected by the Lord himself during his brief ministry in Palestine. They were much like the fifty-five patriots who signed Colonial America's *Declaration of Independence:* targeted men, hunted down by those who opposed their innovative teaching, and destined for persecution, if not a martyr's death.

Unspeakable mistreatment of early Christians, both by the Romans and the Jewish leaders, resulted in a "holy flight" of converts who scattered into all parts of the Western world (Acts 8:1-4). Evangelism was successful, in part, because of the dispersion of these believers in places where the name of Jesus was virtually unknown. In many instances, the story of the cross and the resurrection settled on fertile soil, and new congregations of the church took root.

Having accepted Jesus as Lord and Savior, Christian disciples had a passion to reach lost souls with the message of his saving grace. They trusted in God and his promises and felt called by the gospel of Jesus Christ to live faithfully in their master's service. Their message, fueled by truth and traditions handed down one generation to the next, was patterned after the teaching of apostolic leaders. These zealots were relentless in their quest to make disciples of all nations of the world. Christianity made its way to the northern coast of Africa during the first century and likely appeared in the British Isles, land occupied by the Celts and Druids, late in the first century or shortly thereafter.

Now, fast-forward a hundred or more years and imagine yourself being a Christian in Rome in the early third century. The apostles were dead, as were several generations of Christians who suffered through the persecutions of Nero and his successors, rulers who had little regard for this "sect of the Jews." Letters from early church leaders and the writings of church historian Eusebius (b. circa 260) recount many stories of Roman persecution.

The Reign of Roman Emperors Who Persecuted Christians During the Church's Infancy

NERO	54 AD - 68 AD (years of reign)
Emperor during Paul's Roman imprisonment	
DOMITIAN	81-95
Emperor during John's writing of Revelation	
TRAJAN	98-117
Ignatius, bishop of Antioch, was put to death	
MARCUS AURELIUS	161-180
Christian philosopher Justin was martyred	
SEPTIMIUS SEVERUS	193-211
Forbade conversions to Christianity; heavy persecution in Egypt	

If you had been a child growing up in the third century, perhaps your grandmother would have shared stories of how your great-grandfather and other relatives were captured, tormented, and thrown onto the floor of the Coliseum in Rome to battle with lions and other wild beasts—hardly the kind of story that would allow you to sleep well at night. Christians during this era were burned alive, slain by a Roman sword, or nailed to a cross in the same manner in which Jesus was executed.

At this time, the miraculous spiritual gifts, once used by the apostles and other Christian leaders to confirm the words of divinely inspired revelation, were no longer evident in the churches. As Simon the Sorcerer had observed in Samaria during the first century, it was by "the laying on of the *apostles' hands*" that men were imbued with miraculous gifts of the Holy Spirit (Acts 8:18). Now that the apostles were no longer living to impart such gifts, disciples had to rely on other means to determine what had been ordained by God and what was purely of man's design.

Writings of the apostolic leaders were being gathered into a New Testament canon, but disagreements occurred about which books were suitable for inclusion. Historians cite 367, when Athanasius, a bishop from Alexandria, compiled a list that included the twenty-seven books in the precise order we have today, as the date when this monumental task was completed. No one had his own leather-bound King James Version of the New Testament to search for Paul's teachings or Peter's exhortations. Passages from their epistles did exist, however, and these documents were copied and circulated among the churches for public reading and study. The authoritative instruction from the apostles was revered by church leaders wherever Christianity had taken root.

Apostolic Admonition for Christians to Adhere to Divinely Inspired Instruction

PAUL	REFERENCE 2 TIMOTHY 2:2
"And the things that you have heard from me among many witnesses, commit these to faithful men who will be able to teach others also."	
PAUL	2 TIMOTHY 4:3-4
"For the time will come when they will not endure sound doctrine, but according to their own desires, because they have itching ears, they will heap up for themselves teachers; and they will turn their ears away from the truth, and be turned aside to fables."	
PAUL	2 CORINTHIANS 11:2
"Now I praise you, brethren, that you remember me in all things and keep the traditions just as I have delivered them to you."	
PAUL	2 THESSALONIANS 2:15
"Therefore, brethren, stand fast and hold the traditions which you were taught, whether by word or our epistle."	

PETER	2 PETER 3:1-3

"Beloved, I now write to you this second epistle...that you might be mindful of the words which were spoken before by the holy prophets, and of the commandment of us, the apostles of the Lord and Savior, knowing this first: that scoffers will come in the last days, walking according to their own lusts..."

JOHN	1 JOHN 2:3-4

"Now by this we know that we know him, if we keep his commandments. He who says, 'I know him,' and does not keep his commandments, is a liar, and the truth is not in him."

JOHN	1 JOHN 2:24

"Therefore let that abide in you which you heard from the beginning. If what you heard from the beginning abides in you, you also will abide in the Son and in the Father."

Fortified by these apostolic admonitions and others, Christians conferred with one another to keep the early church in compliance with the teachings of their fathers and their fathers' fathers.

Of course, occasions arose when congregations, being autonomously governed bodies under the guidance of local leaders, differed on key doctrinal issues. Even the first century church had to work through differences on whether circumcision would be binding upon Christians. A meeting was convened in Jerusalem (Acts 15), where the apostles declared that the physical mark in the flesh that identified God's people under the old covenant was not binding upon those believers who were under the new covenant of Jesus Christ. When conferencing appeared to be an appropriate avenue for resolving disputes, other councils were convened in subsequent years to address doctrinal differences among the churches in local regions.

After the apostles passed from the scene, younger Christian leaders took their place, urging believers to withstand persecution from outside their ranks, while maintaining peace within the church community. Clement of Rome, Ignatius of Antioch, and Polycarp of Smyrna were highly regarded bishops in the second century. From writings by their contemporaries, it is believed that all three church leaders suffered a martyr's death.

In addition to the persecution by Roman authorities, strife among the disciples was an ongoing concern for church leaders. Clement wrote a letter to the church in Corinth toward the close of the first century. He took exception to the conflicts that continued to plague this troubled congregation, petitioning the Lord to "restore" the practice of brotherly love among its members.

"Let us therefore, with all haste, put an end to this [state of things]; and let us fall down before the Lord, and beseech him with tears, that he would mercifully be reconciled to us, and restore us to our former seemly and holy practice of brotherly love."
(The First Epistle of Clement, Bishop of Rome, circa 97)

Clement was among the earliest post-apostolic writers to recognize the need for restoring a wayward church, but he was hardly the last. Restoration was a recurring theme among the Ante-Nicene writers, many of who called upon Christians to return to their moorings and to the teaching of the original apostles.

In 325, Emperor Constantine, formerly a successful Roman general who had sympathetic feelings for Christians and their God, convened a council of 318 church leaders at his vacation home in Nicea, Bithynia. His purpose was to restore peace by settling a few doctrinal differences that existed among the congregations scattered throughout the Roman Empire. Most notably, a group led by Arius of Alexandria believed Jesus Christ to be a lesser deity than God the Father. The consensus at Nicea was that the Son and the Father were of equal standing, coexistent except for the years the Son spent on earth. The bishops also settled upon a Sunday as being the proper day for the observance of Easter, an annual event that gained early traction among Christians. The holiday festival included a meal that was reminiscent of the Jewish Passover but with less ritualism and fewer dietary restrictions.

Although not an immersed Christian himself, Constantine tucked the Christian religion under his regime as if it were a new bureau in his administration, treating it as one among several approved metaphysical faiths. What began in the minds of many as an upstart Jewish heresy had now come under an umbrella of protection within the mighty Roman Empire. The church gradually became "Romanized"; the Romans, doing what they often did with any new body of knowledge, codified key elements of the new philosophy and blended the new moral values into its own civil codes.

Doctrinal conclusions agreed upon at Nicea and at subsequent council gatherings eventually became creeds, stipulating the acceptable tenets of belief for those of the Christian faith. It would be difficult for any Christian to find fault with the principal affirmations made at Nicea. "We believe in one God, the Father Almighty,… And one Lord, Jesus Christ,… We believe also in one Holy Spirit…." Over time, however, these creeds, more than Scripture, became the ultimate "test of fellowship" among the believers and were recognized as such at the highest levels of Roman government.

J. Terry Johnson

The years from the Council of Nicea in 325 until the Council of Chalcedon in 451 are known as the "Age of the Great Church Fathers." Augustine (354 – 430), a North African priest who wrote scholarly volumes explaining and defending church doctrine, was a remarkable intellect. His thoughts on grace and original sin were cited centuries later by church reformers Thomas Aquinas (1225 – 1274) and John Calvin (1509 – 1564). He taught that Adam's fall in the Garden of Eden and the sin passed down from one generation to the next make it virtually impossible for any mortal to act responsibly in moral matters. Only God's grace offers hope. In his *Confessions*, Augustine opined, "For what am I to myself without You, but a guide to my own downfall."

Jerome (340 – 420), a linguist who translated the Scripture into Latin, and Eusebius (260 – 340), the best contemporary church historian of this era, contributed valuable writings that added legitimacy to Christianity and its growing body of adherents. Roman Emperor Theodosius, who reigned from 379 – 395, expanded the "privileged status" that Constantine had granted to Christianity, making it the official religion of the Empire. The "Jewish sect" had risen to higher prominence than first century Christians meeting in Roman catacombs could have possibly imagined.

Under a civil government protectorate, Christians suffered less public persecution but lost some of their independence. Caesar, and those who curried his favor, began to set the agenda for the church and its role within the Empire. A hierarchy of leadership had begun to emerge by the early second century: local bishops ceding some of their congregational autonomy to bishops of higher standing in key cities scattered throughout the Roman world. Ignatius, who wrote several epistles to congregations, was the first to call for special respect to be awarded single bishops who happened to enjoy preeminence in their respective communities.

"Take care to do all things in harmony with God, with the bishop presiding in the place of God, and with the presbyters in the place of the council of apostles, and with the deacons, who are most dear to me, entrusted with the business of Jesus Christ,..." (Letter to the Magnesians 2, 6:1)

In time, the bishop of Rome was accepted as first among his peers, and the papacy materialized. That which began as a simple, duplicable system of local congregations springing up in those places where the good news of Jesus Christ was preached gave way to a sophisticated structure of centralized authority, led by a clergy that was more and more removed from the people. Restoration was not in vogue. Expediency and politics trumped authenticity, and the early signs of human manipulation of church government became more apparent.

3

Events Leading to the Great Schism

450 – 1054

Depending upon your point of view, the church either matured into a powerful and substantial organization in the last half of the first millennium, or it drifted into shameful apostasy. The modest move by Emperor Constantine to exercise central control over the church developed into a flood of proclamations and edicts, resulting in greater ecclesiastical power being vested in Rome. In time, as the political influence of Rome began to wane in Europe, the titular head of the Roman Church, the pope, gained even more sway in directing the affairs of his constituents' everyday lives.

Two important events occurred in the fifth and sixth centuries that shaped both the church's present and its future. Gothic tribes from north of the Alps invaded Italy, ultimately bringing an end to any viable reign of the immense political empire that had emanated from Rome. Constantinople, which had been given prominence a century and a half earlier when Emperor Constantine had made this eastern city his capital (330 – 337), became the new seat of political influence. Church leaders representing the Eastern Roman Empire (Constantinople) and those from the Western Roman Empire (Rome) began jockeying for position between the two capitals. The political split set in motion ecclesiastical tension between the major regions, with Rome retaining a slight upper hand by virtue of its long tradition of being recognized as "first among peers."

The second momentous event of the late sixth century was the birth of Muhammad (circa 570) in Arabia. His claim of having had visions from Allah, the name by which Muhammad knew God, gave rise to a new book of scriptures called the Quran. Islam, led by zealots seeking to conquer all non-believing infidels by capturing their cities in the name of Allah, emerged as a competing religious movement to the traditional Judeo-Christian values that had become popular in the West. Damascus fell in 635, Jerusalem succumbed in 638, and all of Egypt was under Islamic control by 642. This turn of events was an early precursor for almost two hundred years of Crusades (1095 – 1272) led by armies sent to the Middle East to reclaim territory under the banner of Christianity.

Over a period of five hundred years, laboring first through unspeakable persecution and later suffering the fall of its governmental protectorate, the Roman Church morphed into something quite different from what it had been at the close of the first century. Autonomous congregations, led by local bishops and deacons, became assimilated into a federated church that spread its tentacles to the far corners of the Roman Empire. Under the direction of professional clerics, new traditions pertaining to church governance and worship were adopted. Subsequently, these innovative practices were codified into ecclesiastical creeds and were treated with the same sense of importance as the original doctrines and traditions espoused by the apostles.

No single change was of greater significance than the emergence of the papacy and the central administration that grew up around the papal office. From the simplicity of what the apostle Peter described as "a holy priesthood," in which all Christians had access to God through a single mediator, Jesus Christ (1 Peter 2:5), a multi-tiered bureaucracy of professional priests came into the picture. A distinct line of demarcation existed between these priests (clergy) and the people (laity). Before the end of the first millennium, taxes to support the pope and his subordinates were extracted from local church coffers. Corporal punishment was used to deal with those who dared to defy the creeds that grew out of ecclesiastical councils, and armies were assembled by the heads of church and state to confront the spread of Islam in the Middle East. The church had become a powerful militant force in Europe and throughout the Mediterranean Basin.

By the turn of the first millennium, the acrimony between the Roman Church and the Byzantine Church (Constantinople) had hit the breaking point. Fundamental differences, dating back hundreds of years, separated the two ecclesiastical powers. An event that had caused exceptional angst was the role that Pope Leo III had played in 800 when he crowned Charlemagne, King of the Franks, as the new emperor of the Holy Roman Empire. This was an affront to the Byzantine emperor, who exercised considerable influence over the Eastern Church and its patriarch. Differences between the two church bodies eventually boiled over, and in 1054 an open breach, commonly known as the "Great Schism" or "The East-West Schism," occurred.

The principal figures in the schism were Pope Leo IX of Rome, along with his legate Cardinal Humbert, and Constantinople's Patriarch Michael Cerularius. The patriarch had defiantly challenged the Roman Church's tradition of using unleavened bread in the observance of the Eucharist (Lord's Supper), claiming it was Jewish tradition rather than an approved Christian practice to use the unleavened bread. When he proceeded to close the Roman churches in Constantinople, Pope Leo IX was outraged. He sent Cardinal Humbert to meet with Cerularius, but the meeting never took place. Instead, Humbert left a papal bull, an edict from Pope Leo himself, at the high altar of the Cathedral Church of St. Sophia in Constantinople. The edict excommunicated the Eastern patriarch, who responded with a similar denouncement of the Western Church. For all practical purposes, the leadership of the two church factions had excommunicated one another, each claiming the other had led his communicants away from the "true church."

Although not commonly recognized as a "restoration movement," the Great Schism had some of that flavor. Both church bodies claimed to hold the high ground, accusing the other side of imposing man-made traditions upon the people. The Eastern Church could no longer abide innovations that had crept into the Roman Catholic Church's liturgy, and the Eastern leaders chafed under the growing display of power exercised by the Roman pope. Language and cultural differences also contributed to the division of the two church communities, making compromise difficult to achieve.

In addition to its charge of abusive papal authority, the Eastern Church objected to a growing list of modernisms introduced by Rome. Specifically, it rejected the teaching about an intermediate state of the deceased called Purgatory, it took strong exception to the doctrine of Mary's Immaculate Conception, and it did not accept Rome's insertion of the phrase *filioque* ("and from the Son") into the Nicene Creed of 325. The insertion, which had occurred hundreds of years earlier without ecumenical approval, suggested that the Holy Spirit proceeded both from God the Father and from Christ the Son. The Eastern Church held that the Holy Spirit proceeded solely from God the Father, citing Jesus' own words in John 15:26.

The Orthodox Church also refused to recognize sprinkling as baptism, holding to the apostolic practice of baptizing by immersion. Its own practice was to immerse a person three times: once in the name of the Father, once in the name of the Son, and a third time in the name of the Holy Spirit.

The Orthodox Church abhorred the Roman Church's introduction of musical instruments into the worship assembly, a practice that, according to most credible church historians, did not develop until the mid to late seventh century when Pope Vitalian (657 – 672) introduced the organ as a fixture for celebrating the public mass. Continuing into the twenty-first century, Orthodox churches in many parts of the world have maintained the practice of acapella singing, believing the use of instruments of music to be an erroneous addition by their Roman brethren.

Both East and West churches built hierarchical infrastructure into their priesthoods. The pinnacle position in Rome was the pope; in Constantinople, it was the patriarch. Priests in the East were allowed to marry but forbidden to shave their beards, while those in the Roman Church could be clean-shaven but were required to remain celibate. Priests filled a variety of duties that included both public and private functions. They led the worship services that had become increasingly formal and filled with ritualism. The Roman Church conducted its public mass using Latin exclusively as the language of the church. The Orthodox Church services had less formality and used Greek as the language of choice.

Primary Issues that Divided the Roman Catholic Church and the Eastern Orthodox Church

ROMAN CHURCH	BYZANTINE (EASTERN) CHURCH
PAPACY	
Pope in Rome was universal leader; infallible in ecclesiastical pronouncements	Patriarch in Constantinople was a peer of the Pope in Rome; Roman Pope was not a universal, infallible leader of the church (2 CORINTHIANS 11:2)
PURGATORY	
Taught there was an intermediary place where the dead could atone for earthly sins	Did not accept Roman Church's position on purgatory
IMMACULATE CONCEPTION	
Taught that Mary was without sin	Did not accept Roman Church's position on Immaculate Conception
THE BREAD USED IN THE SACRAMENTAL MASS	
Bread unleavened, as when Jesus instituted the Lord's Supper	Used leavened bread to celebrate the Lord's Supper
INSTRUMENTS OF MUSIC	
Used instruments of music in the mass after they were introduced in mid to late seventh century	Did not use instruments of music in worship assemblies

BAPTISM	
Changed from immersion to sprinkling	Baptized by immersing each candidate three times
PRIESTS	
Priests must remain celibate; not required to have beards	Priests allowed to marry but could not shave beards
LANGUAGE	
Mass conducted in Latin	Greek language used in worship assemblies
NICENE CREED	
Rome inserted word *filioque* into Nicene Creed to suggest Holy Spirit had proceeded from both God the Father and the Son (John 14-16)	Held that Rome had erroneously changed the Nicene Creed by inserting the word *filioque* and had done so without the consent of other ecclesiastical authorities

Other issues divided the two churches. They did not agree on dates and methods for observing Easter and Christmas. The Roman Church had also established its list of *sacraments*, or holy activities, that were critical to one's salvation, whereas the Eastern Church felt it was an abomination to add any meritorious works to God's offer of salvation by grace through faith. By the time of the Great Schism, many human traditions had been incorporated into the two opposing churches' creeds of faith. In what might be called a weak attempt to restore New Testament teaching regarding the church, each faction called upon the other to correct its errant positions, but neither body was a true reflection of the first century apostolic church. Restoration had become a process of taking two steps forward and three steps back.

4

The Church Goes to War

1054 - 1250

In the eleventh, twelfth, and thirteenth centuries, a common cause brought the Roman Catholic Church and the Eastern Orthodox Church closer together than they might otherwise have expected. Christians, whether affiliated with the Roman Church in the West or the Byzantine church in the East, grew alarmed with the Muslim occupation in Palestine. Pilgrimages to Jerusalem were becoming more dangerous for Christians, and access to shrines and landmark sites was being denied to pilgrims on a regular basis.

The tipping point came when an army of Muslims known as the Seljuk Turks, who were migrating from Persia, moved within striking distance of Constantinople. The Byzantines viewed the new enemy as a threat similar to the marauding Huns that had hastened the collapse of the Roman Empire. Byzantine armies had brought back tales of unspeakable atrocities perpetrated by the menacing Turks.

When the Turkish encroachment threatened the Byzantine Empire itself, Emperor Alexios I Komnenos sent a plea for help to his counterparts in Rome. Something had to be done to halt the Muslim aggression and to remove any threat of danger for Christians who wished to travel to Palestine. Without trying to reconcile religious differences between East and West, Pope Urban II accepted the invitation to raise an army of Western Europeans who would "take up the cross" in battle against Muslims, the splintered churches' common enemy.

To some extent, Urban was successful in raising an army of thousands by offering redemptive incentives to those who chose to participate. He viewed the conflict with the Muslims as a "just war" being waged to redress the persecution Christians had suffered for centuries at the hands of militant Arabs and Turks. Crusaders were promised remission of sins for making the journey, and, for those who died in combat, the pope promised immediate entry into heaven. Within a year, a massive army was organized, possibly as many as 100,000 men, and the First Crusade, bound initially for Constantinople and then the Middle East, launched on August 15, 1096, from various cities in France and Italy.

Although history records many Crusades organized over the next five centuries, the first four, occurring from 1095 until 1204, were by far the most significant. From a military point of view, the Crusades were nominally successful. The First Crusade drove the Muslim resistance away from Constantinople and liberated Jerusalem, opening the city to a more hospitable environment for Christian pilgrims. An uneasy coexistence between Muslims, Jews, and Christian occupiers ensued, lasting almost fifty years, when Muslims began to reconquer cities that had been lost during the siege of the First Crusade.

Upon learning of Muslim aggression and the loss of previously conquered Palestinian territory, clerics in Western Europe called for the Second Crusade. French and German armies reached Jerusalem in 1147 but failed to regain lands under Muslim control. On a brighter side for the Christian Crusaders, the Muslim occupation in Spain and Portugal, parts of Northern Africa, and numerable islands in the Mediterranean was diminished because of a series of military engagements.

Forty years later, Saladin, a Kurdish leader who became the First Sultan of Egypt and Syria, organized a loosely federated group of Muslims and recaptured most of the cities previously conquered by the first two Crusades. Distraught by this news, Pope Gregory VIII called for a Third Crusade, this one designed to reestablish Christian control throughout Palestine. Heads of state from France and Germany, along with England's King Richard I, also known as Richard the Lion-Hearted, led their armies hundreds of miles to the Bible lands. Except for retaking a few small coastal towns and making a pact with Saladin that allowed Christians to make their pilgrimages to Jerusalem, little was accomplished.

The last of the four major Crusades was also an ill-fated effort. Pope Innocent III called for a campaign in 1202, seeking to reoccupy the critical Palestinian cities and driving the Muslims away from Christian shrines and "holy" sites. After encountering problems financing the original plan, the Fourth Crusade ended in Constantinople, where the Crusaders sacked the city in 1204 and set up a Latin Empire that was designed to restore Western European control over the Byzantine territory. Whereas the threat of a common enemy might have provided an opportunity to bring the two church factions together, the Western encampment inside the Byzantine realm actually drove the two churches further apart.

At least three major developments growing out of the Crusades had a lasting impact upon the nature and behavior of the church. First, the church became much more militaristic. Can you imagine the church in the twenty-first century calling upon its members to bear arms in order to advance its agenda? This is the bride of Jesus Christ—the same Jesus who told Peter to put up his sword in the Garden of Gethsemane; Jesus who taught his disciples to love their enemies; Jesus who laid down his own life, praying for those who had schemed the diabolical plot to kill him. Yet it was the leadership of the church during the Middle Ages that called for "holy war" and caused thousands of innocent Jews and Muslims to die by the sword of war-faring Christian Crusaders.

This same militaristic fervor that was used to war against Arab and Turk infidels was later redirected to support the church in its efforts to punish heretics. It was not as if the Crusades marked the first time that brute force was used to address enemies of the church, but the experience of having assembled an army to do the church's bidding appeared to embolden Roman clerics to do something similar as a means of curtailing local skirmishes with heretics. Toward the end of the Crusades, believers accused of practices or views that were contrary to the church's established creed were treated with hostile force, often resulting in corporal punishment, dismemberment, or death.

In 1209, Pope Innocent III launched an armed Crusade that lasted twenty years. Its expressed objective was not to slay the sons of Muhammad but to eradicate French dissidents, known as Cathari (or Albigensians), who sought to revive moral and spiritual purity within the church. The Cathari were not true restorers, never intending to take the church back to its apostolic roots, but they did call for changes to be made within the church and were persecuted for their defiance of the authorities in Rome. Pope Innocent IV sanctioned the use of torture in 1252 to assist inquisitors who demanded confessions from suspected heretics.

A second occurrence that gained acceptance during the Crusades was the practice of issuing indulgences—meritorious works that were touted as having the power to atone for sins. When Pope Urban II recruited the army for the First Crusade, he made a series of impassioned speeches, offering remission of sins to those who fought in these battles and an immediate home in heaven for those who died as martyrs. He either failed to grasp that salvation for Christians has always been a matter of God's grace, coupled with the atoning blood of a loving Savior, or he used the "bait" merely as a ruse to recruit an army. Either way, his offer was nothing more than selling indulgences to the highest bidders, and it set the stage for heightened abuse of this practice. Centuries later, nothing infuriated Christian reformers more than dealing with the church's henchmen who preyed upon the weak and guilt-ridden by selling them ineffective indulgences.

Finally, the Crusades resulted in enormous wealth being bestowed on the Roman Church. Appeals were made to affluent land barons to fund the Crusades by making gifts of realty or other valuable properties to the church. Some responded to this plea by offering their treasures in lieu of taking the personal risk of bearing arms. The result was that the church incurred fortune beyond anything it had known before. With new riches came greater stature and power as the church conducted its business with nobles, kings, and other heads of state.

Wealth, however, can be a two-edged sword. The "glorious church" that was meant to reflect the humility and goodness of its Lord and Master became bloated with riches and appeared arrogant to the common man. Even the clerics were suspicious and jealous of the church's enormous affluence and became critical of the disparity between the leadership that seemed to live off the wealth vis-à-vis the masses that had virtually nothing. The seeds of reformation were sown into the hearts of a few outspoken critics, who, over a period of the next three hundred years, would turn the church upside down with demands for reform.

Before leaving this era, mention must be made of the Scholastic movement that set the stage for church reform. At one time, historians referred to the centuries between the fall of Rome (fifth century) and the early stirrings of the renaissance (fourteenth century) as the "Dark Ages." The term depicted a vast timespan that was not known for its contemporary historical records and expressions of art or scientific achievement.

As historians have learned more about these disparaged times, less is said about them being the "Dark Ages," and more favor is credited to them for the work of a few notable scholars who prepared the way for church reformers in subsequent centuries. Anselm of Canterbury, England (1033 – 1109); Peter Abelard of France (1079 – 1142); and Thomas Aquinas, a Dominican monk from Italy (1225 – 1274), were all preeminent leaders in the rise of Scholasticism, a movement that provided a support of religious faith by the use of logic and philosophical thought.

Aquinas's *Summa Theologiae*, a compilation of articles that answered hundreds of theological questions, continues to have influence in shaping dogma within the Roman Catholic Church. His writings provided a rational basis by which everyday church practices could be explained and defended. This included the church's teaching on the papacy, penance, the sacraments, indulgences, and transubstantiation—the presence of Christ in the bread and the wine during the observance of the Lord's Supper. His work and the writings of other Scholastic clerics became benchmark documents for the men who gave rise to major church reform.

5

The Groundwork for Reformation

1250 - 1450

Following the Great Schism, the annals of religious history are filled with names of groups and individuals that made an effort to correct doctrinal error and abusive leadership practices in the Roman Catholic Church. Some of these dissidents, men who could not abide ecclesiastical corruption, are nothing more than a footnote in church history. In the twelfth century, Peter Waldo was such a man.

Waldo, a merchant from Lyons, France, gave up his wealth to live a simple life without the distractions of affluence. The New Testament was the sole authority for his personal religious beliefs. He preferred a church service led by laymen who preached in the vernacular rather than the ritualism of a formal Latin mass. The Roman Church was wary of harm that could be done by allowing uneducated clerics the opportunity to preach at will. Waldo and his band of brothers, the Waldensians, were eventually excommunicated. They lived in the mountains of France and were often in hiding from church enforcers that carried out the pope's will to eradicate their heretical movement.

A perfect storm began to brew, culminating in an illuminating era known as the Protestant Reformation. The activists were primarily "reformers," not "restorers." Their corrective attempts were intended to purify the church by working within its existing structure. An effort to restore the church to its apostolic roots was, for most of them, beyond their visionary constraints.

Nonetheless, these outspoken critics were brave men and women who risked excommunication, imprisonment, and the threat of death in order to influence religious changes during their lifetimes. Without their voices of reason, later attempts to restore the New Testament church would have been far more difficult. This unfolding story of tracing the church from its roots to the present cannot be told properly without saluting the substantial contributions made by leaders of the Protestant Reformation and those who prepared the ground in advance of this historic movement.

John Wycliffe (1324 – 1384)

John Wycliffe of England has frequently been called "the Morning Star of the Reformation." Although he lived almost two hundred years prior to the Protestant Reformation, Wycliffe set an example that emboldened later spokesmen who lobbied church leaders to make doctrinal and ceremonial changes. An educated man who taught at Oxford, Wycliffe was a layman who took great exception to the papacy's exercise of unrestrained authority over men such as himself—men who desired to preach the gospel in their own language.

Wycliffe challenged the legitimacy of the papacy and its control over the spiritual affairs of the people. He believed that the Scripture was the ultimate authority for one's faith in God and that it was sufficient to lead Christians into all truth. He abhorred what he believed to be flagrant abuses by the clergy, having no use for those who sought refuge in monastic life.

Among Wycliffe's most enduring legacies was his translation of the Bible into English from the Latin Vulgate (Jerome's translation from the late fourth century). He has not been credited with having personally translated all sixty-six books of the Bible, but he did translate the gospels and led the two-year campaign that resulted in the English Wycliffe Bible, which was completed in 1384, the year of his death. The new translation made it easier for his disciples to fulfill their dreams of preaching to the people in their native tongue.

Those who identified with Wycliffe's defiance of the pope and sought to emulate his style of preaching became known as Lollards, a derisive term meant to cast aspersion on those who preached without official sanction from the Roman Church. The Lollards, who lasted as a loosely federated body in England for almost two hundred years, were more of a nuisance to the Roman Church than they were a threat. In their sermons, they encouraged the practice of reading the Bible in the English language, and they upbraided the Catholic Church for its preoccupation with amassing wealth. Later popes branded them as heretics, executing some of their more outspoken followers by burning them at the stake and driving members of the sect underground. When the Protestant Reformation took root in England in the sixteenth century, the Lollards were absorbed into the movement.

Late in his life, Wycliffe had a series of confrontations with the Roman Church that might have led to his excommunication had it not been for the protection of John of Gaunt, the uncle and advisor to the English king Richard II. Pope Gregory XI was unsuccessful in getting the English throne to control Wycliffe, but the pope did have enough influence on the administration at Oxford to strip Wycliffe of his teaching position at the university. The pope died without having pronounced a formal censure on Wycliffe, and the reformer moved forward with his biblical translation project. Thirty years after his death, Wycliffe was formally excommunicated for the heretical influence he once had on the Lollards and others of similar persuasion. The pope ordered that Wycliffe's remains be exhumed and cremated.

John Hus (1369 – 1415)

Among the most ardent disciples of John Wycliffe was John Hus, a Bohemian priest who taught at the University of Prague. Hus admired Wycliffe's insistence that laymen be allowed to preach the gospel in a common language rather than being bound by the church's tradition of using Latin exclusively in the public assemblies. Hus translated some of Wycliffe's books into the Czech language and preached from the Scripture in his native tongue.

Hus believed the New Testament to be the exclusive guide for the church on all matters of doctrine and practice. He emulated the simple lifestyle of Jesus and chose to live without personal treasure. Among his many reforms, Hus reintroduced the wine into the observance of the Eucharist (Lord's Supper).

When Pope Alexander V issued a papal bull in 1410 that ordered all of the writings of John Wycliffe to be gathered and burned, Hus took strong exception to the pope's order, resulting in his own excommunication from the church. From this point until his death in 1415, Hus spoke forcefully against the abusive edicts of the pope and the immoral behavior of the Roman Catholic priests. He condemned the pope's use of brutality to uphold his papal bulls, and he attacked the church's practice of selling indulgences to congregants in exchange for their personal atonement. Hus taught vigorously that forgiveness came from genuine repentance and could not be bought with any amount of currency.

Charges were brought against Hus in 1414, labeling him a heretic and a candidate for execution. A trial was held the next spring, and Hus was found guilty of the charges. Unless he had been willing to recant, he was to be sentenced to death. Hus made concessions where he could but would not step back from the major positions he had held against the practice of selling indulgences and the immoral behavior of the priesthood. In July 1415, slightly more than one hundred years prior to Martin Luther's prime years in Wittenberg, John Hus, an early leader of church reform, was burned at the stake.

Two factions emerged among those who were followers of Hus: one group, the Taborites, would not accept any church practice that was not *expressly authorized in the Scripture*; the other faction, the Ultraquists, accepted any church practice *unless it had been expressly condemned in the Scripture*. The Moravian Church, which claims for itself the moniker "First Protestant Church," traces its origins to John Hus.

———

In the late fifteenth century, the key elements for the "perfect storm" began to swirl into a powerful tempest that became known by historians as the Protestant Reformation. Seeds of ecclesiastical change had been sown by Wycliffe, Hus, the Lollards, and other devoted reformers for almost two hundred years. These well-intentioned critics found fault with the egregious behavior of church leaders, took strong exception to the church's raising funds through the selling of indulgences, and advocated that Latin no longer be the exclusive language of the church.

A host of political, economic, and social changes also set the stage for the church's impending transformation. Feudalism was on the wane, and nobles whose provinces had been paying papal taxes to underwrite Crusades and other church activities were not as willing to pay the assessments. Nationalism was on the rise, resulting in kings becoming more aggressive in building their respective power bases and less amenable to sharing that power with Rome. The early stages of a renaissance that brought learning and enlightenment to the masses encouraged the nobility to think more independently than they had done in the past, resulting in less willingness to do the bidding of the pope and his envoys. And the development of moveable type, the key to Johannes Gutenberg being able to create his innovative printing press, allowed a more practical means of getting the Scripture into the hands of laymen in their own languages.

Adding to this improbable tempest was the unseemly behavior of the Roman Catholic Church and its leaders. In many quarters of Europe, the priesthood had become compromised by its own self-absorption, its high-minded directives, its greedy assessments, its cruel punishment of critics, and its scandalous moral behavior.

The open study of Scripture had been replaced with ritualism and creeds. Above all, the Roman Church held firm to the seven "sacraments"—rituals of the highest priority because their origin had come from specific examples of Christ's ministry while he was on earth. The church taught that participating in these sacraments brought Christians in close proximity to God and his gracious blessings. The seven sacraments were—and still are today—baptism, confirmation, the Eucharist (or Holy Communion), penance, matrimony, holy orders, and the anointing of the sick and dying.

Over time, the self-sacrificing practice of performing "good works" mutated into "meritorious works" as a means of achieving personal atonement. For those who preferred not to perform such works of penance, the church made an accommodation by aggressively selling indulgences, which were nothing more than meritorious works of a different type. Critics seized upon these practices, declaring that remission of sins now could be purchased for a price.

6

The Protestant Reformation

1450 - 1564

Martin Luther (1483 – 1546)

The one person most frequently identified with the Protestant Reformation is Martin Luther. Born in Germany to parents of low-to-middle income, Luther left his study of law to enter a monastery and, at the age of twenty-four, was ordained as a priest in the Roman Catholic Church. Receiving encouragement from his superiors, Luther decided to become a professor of theology at the University of Wittenberg. In 1512, five years after taking his vows, he received his Doctor of Theology degree, qualifying him to lecture at the university on the Bible and related subjects. He became an accomplished lecturer and a popular professor with his students.

Having developed a strong conviction that man's justification was a gift of God's grace, Luther detested the church's practice of raising financial support by selling indulgences. He lectured on the subject frequently, always taking the opportunity to denounce the promotion of meritorious works and the sale of indulgences. In 1517 Luther completed a document known informally as his "Ninety-Five Theses," which addressed the issue of indulgences. Whether the legend that he nailed his theses to the door of the All-Saints' (Castle) Church in Wittenberg is correct or not, the translation of his paper from Latin into German received wide circulation, bringing him unexpected notoriety among established church leaders, including Pope Leo X.

Luther was a prolific writer. He wrote a brief commentary on Galatians; penned the words and composed the melody to the popular hymn "A Mighty Fortress Is Our God"; translated the Bible into German; and developed religious instructions (cate-chisms) to make the sacraments and other rituals more under-standable to the people in the pew.

Although it was never Luther's intention to break from the Ro-man Catholic Church and begin a church of his own persuasion, he spent the last twenty-five years of his life excoriating the Roman Church. He insisted that the Scripture alone was the authority for Christian belief, debunking the Roman Church's practice of ele-vating traditions and papal interpretations to the same level as the biblical accounts. Luther taught that all believers comprised the priesthood of Jesus Christ and that their justification was by faith, not meritorious works or the payment of indulgences. Refusing to recant his writings, Luther was excommunicated from the Roman Catholic Church in January 1521.

Holy Roman Emperor Charles V presided in a civil trial be-fore magistrates in Worms to determine any consequences for the reformer's outspoken charges against the church. Luther took his stand, railing against the many traditions that had corrupted the Roman Church and had become binding upon the believers. "Un-less I am refuted and convicted by testimonies of the Scriptures or by clear arguments…I cannot and will not recant anything," Luther said in his defense. At the conclusion of the hearings in May 1521, Luther's writings were officially banned and he himself was deemed to be an outlaw of the state. Only by the assistance of Frederick III, Duke of Saxony, was Luther's life spared from those who sought to enforce the ruling at Worms. Two years later, Luther shed his vows of celibacy and married Katharina von Bora, a former nun.

Among Luther's closest faculty contemporaries at the University of Wittenberg was Philipp Melanchthon, a Greek scholar. The two professors banded together, accepting their lots as outcasts of the Roman Catholic Church, and set the groundwork for a new church that ultimately took Luther's name as its moniker. It was Melanchthon who wrote *The Augsburg Confession*, the document that became the framework for establishing the Lutheran Church.

In hindsight, it is easy to look back on Martin Luther's life and suggest that he didn't take church reform far enough or that he simply gave birth to a new denomination of Christian faith without restoring the church to its apostolic roots. It must be said, however, that Luther was a brave man, risking his reputation, his professional standing, and living most of his adult life in mortal peril from those who had become his enemies. In *On the Babylonian Captivity of the Church*, one of his more passionate writings, Luther courageously likened the exploitations and man-devised traditions of the Roman Catholic Church to the Babylonian Captivity that took the Jews away from the Promised Land.

Luther stood by the courage of his convictions and, in his own way, made giant strides in curbing abuses that had tainted the Roman Catholic Church. He was more of a reformer than a restorer, but he used his God-given talents to put a fresh face on the glorious church of Jesus Christ.

Huldreich Zwingli (1484 – 1531)

Born in Switzerland one year after Martin Luther's birth, Huldreich (or Huldrych) Zwingli was in many respects more successful in reforming the church than his more famous German contemporary. The son of a farmer, young Zwingli was sent from home at age ten to pursue his education. He received his master's degree in 1506 and became a parish priest.

In 1519 Zwingli was appointed priest for the church in Zurich, where he made a name for himself, often standing in open defiance to the corruption within the Roman Church. He placed his faith in the authority of the Scripture, unwilling to accept that the creeds formed in councils or the teachings of church leaders were equivalent to the word of God. The doctrinal changes he advocated were the results of his personal study of the Scripture and the exegetical preaching technique that he used during worship services at the Zurich church.

Among the doctrinal changes Zwingli championed were these: respecting the Scripture as the sole authority for church practices; denying the efficacy of indulgences; Jesus Christ recognized as the sole head of the church; the abolition of icons, relics, and mechanical instruments of music in worship assemblies; the sermon becoming the primary event in worship rather than the traditional Roman Catholic mass; clergy allowed to marry; and observing the Lord's Supper as a more informal memorial feast rather than a ritualistic sacrament that occurred in the church's mass. Zwingli defied conventional thinking in these areas and in other religious practices. He was, by far, more of a restorer than Luther or any other cleric of his day.

Zwingli and Martin Luther had an historic encounter in Marburg, Germany, in 1529. Mutual friends brought the two great reformers together, hoping to establish a single confession of faith among the two rival Protestant camps. After three days of debate and discussions, there was agreement on fourteen of fifteen articles of faith. The point of difference, left unresolved, centered on the practice of the partaking of the Lord's Supper. Zwingli believed the bread and the cup were symbolic figures that signified Christ's body and blood. Luther rejected both Zwingli's symbolic approach and the traditional Roman Church's interpretation of "transubstantiation," in which the bread becomes Christ's body and the wine becomes his blood. He affirmed a position between the two extremes, choosing to believe that the "spiritual presence" of Jesus occurred during the ceremonial event.

Emerging during this same era was a more radical group of Zwingli supporters who broke away from their founder and became known as the Anabaptist movement. Among these was Conrad Grebel (1498 –1526), who took issue with Zwingli on two major issues. First, Grebel believed his mentor was too soft on the need for separation between church administration and governance by the state; second, whereas Zwingli taught that infant baptism was "ineffective," Grebel and his Anabaptist colleagues sought immediate reform on this issue, believing a candidate for baptism must always be old enough to make his own confession of faith. Hostility arose between Zwingli and his former friends, resulting in severe persecution of the Anabaptists both by the Roman Church and the zealots who adhered to Zwingli's more moderate approach to reform.

"Anabaptist," which means "to be baptized anew," was never a name offered in a favorable light. Enemies of the movement used the term derisively, intending to scorn those who refused to baptize their infants. Adherents disdained the moniker, believing adult baptism was the only true baptism and that infant baptism had no spiritual consequence. Consequently, the Anabaptist movement could never survive as a denomination under its own name, but it did give birth to new expressions of Protestant thought that gained great influence in Europe and later in the American colonies. More than anyone of their era, they were genuine restorers of apostolic teaching. Among those growing out of the movement were the Amish, the Mennonites, and various strains of the Baptist Church.

Zwingli died in 1531 during a military encounter against armies from Swiss sub-states, or cantons that opposed the reformer's nontraditional religious beliefs. The thirteen cantons were loosely federated, operating almost as thirteen independent states. As Zwingli's teaching became widespread in Switzerland and other parts of Central Europe, leaders from some of the cantons that were aligned more rigidly with the Roman Church bore arms to crush the heretical teaching. In the process, the voice of Zwingli was silenced, but his revolutionary ideas about the church and its need to look only to the Scripture for its teaching and practices lived on for generations.

John Calvin (1509 – 1564)

Although born and educated in France, John Calvin spent much of his adult years in and around Geneva, Switzerland. His popularity as an educator and a writer came at least half a generation after Zwingli's and Luther's prime years. Their works were known to Calvin and helped shape some of his own theological perspective. All three men, sometimes referred to as the "Three Pillars of the Reformation," elevated the authority of the Scripture over the human traditions and papal decrees that emanated from Rome.

Calvin made his most important contribution to the Reformation with his pen. Perhaps the most gifted religious author since Thomas Aquinas, the renowned scholar who was responsible for articulating the core church doctrines in the thirteenth century (*see chapter four*), Calvin gathered the fresh ideas offered by contemporary theologians and wrote the *Institutes of the Christian Religion* at the age of twenty-seven. This document, revised often over the ensuing years, was a masterful exercise in systematizing Christian doctrine and practices. The central theme of his treatise was the "sovereignty of God."

Owing in part to the enduring nature of the written word, Calvin's influence spread further than either Zwingli's or Luther's. He wrote volumes pertaining to critical Christian studies, including commentaries on many books in the Bible.

A proponent of Augustine's doctrine of "original sin," Calvin believed the fall of Adam in the Garden of Eden ultimately transmitted the guilt of sin to all mankind and did so from the time of each person's birth. *God, being the sovereign ruler that he is, by his omniscience is able to determine those who are destined for heaven and those who are bound for hell.* By God's foreknowledge, salvation and damnation were, therefore, predestined.

With salvation being totally an operation of God, Calvin had no use for those who peddled indulgences. He broke from the Roman Church at an early age, calling for all members of the ecclesiastical community to make major changes. He introduced congregational singing into the church in Geneva and sought broader roles of leadership among elders, deacons, and teachers at the local church level. Calvinism eventually became an international movement, especially influencing the Reformed Church in Europe and the Presbyterian Church in English-speaking countries.

7

Reformation in England and Scotland

1500 - 1620

Until the sixteenth century, England had been reticent to embrace the ecclesiastical reforms being championed by Martin Luther and others on the Continent. John Wycliffe's efforts to resist papal intrusion into the affairs of local churches in England had a small measure of continuing influence from the time of his death in 1384 until King Henry VIII assumed the English throne in 1509. Henry himself was in good standing with the pope, having been named "Defender of the Faith" for his denouncement of Luther's recalcitrant behavior. The much-celebrated king was neither a reformer nor a restorer, but rather an opportunist who used the political climate of his day to advance his personal agenda.

Nationalism was on the rise in many parts of Europe. Kings were empire builders and had little regard for papal bulls and demands for tithes from Rome. When Henry grew tired of waiting for the pope to issue an annulment of his first marriage to Catherine of Aragon, he sought and eventually received an Act of Parliament in 1534, declaring him to be the "supreme head" of the Church of England. Thomas Cranmer, the Archbishop of Canterbury, granted the king his annulment, and the Church of England, looking very much like the Roman Catholic Church, became fully operational.

J. Terry Johnson

Henry was succeeded on the English throne by his only son, Edward VI. During Edward's brief reign (1547 –1553), the Church of England adopted its popular *Book of Common Prayer*. The English Church also made several key revisions to its worship practices, drawing distinctions between its Anglicized observance of mass and the traditional Latin service used in Rome.

Edward's half-sister Mary, pledging her allegiance to Rome, ascended to the throne and began to reverse the Protestant advancement. Persecution of Protestants ensued in cruel fashion, much akin to practices of the Spanish Inquisition, which had been formally sanctioned by the pope in 1542. Among those executed was former Archbishop Cranmer, whose annulment of King Henry's marriage to Catherine had made their daughter Mary an illegitimate child—a loathsome consequence the new queen was unwilling to forgive. Tudor Queen Mary became known to her countrymen and in the annals of history as "Bloody Mary."

Elizabeth I, Henry's second child, the daughter of Anne Boleyn and a half-sister both to Mary, daughter of Catherine, and Edward VI, son of Jane Seymour, was crowned queen of England in 1559. She reigned forty-five years and was the fifth and last of the Tudor monarchs. Elizabeth sought middle ground in the dispute between Protestants and Catholics. The queen refused to recognize the pope's authority over the church in England, but she did accept the ancient creeds (Nicene Creed, Apostles' Creed, etc.) as the basis for church dogma. She also used Parliament to legislate matters pertaining to the church. The Act of Uniformity required all people to attend church services each week or be subject to a fine.

The Church of England punished heretics through the queen's army that was dispatched to the far reaches of the kingdom. Those singled out for discipline included both Catholics, who denied the right of the Church of England to exist apart from Rome, and the radical Protestants, who felt there needed to be a thorough cleansing of the church, seeking to make its separation from Rome even more apparent. The latter developed into a movement known as Puritanism.

During this same era, seeds of reformation were rife in Scotland. The primary spokesman for political freedom was John Knox, a compelling preacher who, while studying in Geneva, had been influenced by John Calvin. He advocated a localized form of church government to be led by bishops, or "presbyters," as opposed to the hierarchical system that governed the churches in Rome and England.

A Reformed Church of Scotland, the forerunner of the Presbyterian Church, was sanctioned by the Scottish Parliament in 1560. Being Calvinistic in its theology, the Church of Scotland found itself at odds with both the Roman Catholic Church and the Church of England. Many of the political issues creating strife between England and Scotland over the next century grew out of their own ecclesiastical differences.

The most aggressive effort to restore New Testament Christianity in England came from the Puritans. Initially, Puritanism was not an identifiable sect of its own, but a movement that existed within established churches, discontent congregants demanding that religious practices be modeled more closely after the teachings of the Scripture. Their appeal was not popular with English royalty, who chose to punish the dissidents rather than adopt church reforms.

Some Puritans, known by this contemptuous term that was originally ascribed to the group by their critics, merely wanted to reform the Church of England. The compromises offered by Queen Elizabeth I were not perceived by these Christians as having gone far enough to correct the centuries of man-induced traditions that had corrupted the Roman Catholic Church and its newly formed English counterpart. Puritanism sought true church reform.

A more aggressive arm of the Puritan movement was convinced that reform was wasted effort. Separatists lobbied for a complete break from the Church of England, restoring both the church and the Christian lifestyle to resemble patterns found in the New Testament. They suffered oppressive persecutions for their outspoken views, causing some to leave England in search of greater religious freedom. Holland became a sanctuary for a small group of Separatists, but their stay was brief. They feared the Dutch culture would become a negative influence on their alien community of faith. It was this group that eventually sailed west in search of a new land. They were the Pilgrims on the *Mayflower,* arriving in Plymouth on the eastern shore of North America in 1620.

Award-winning author Nathaniel Philbrick, in his bestselling historical account, *Mayflower,* described these seventeenth-century Christian mavericks in unmistakable terms.

A Puritan believed it was necessary to venture back to the absolute beginning of Christianity, before the church had been corrupted by centuries of laxity and abuse, to locate divine truth. In lieu of time travel, there was the Bible, with the New Testament providing the only reliable account of Christ's time on earth while the Old Testament provided a rich storehouse of still vital truths. If something was not in the scriptures, it was a man-made distortion of what God intended. At once radical and deeply conservative, the Puritans had chosen to spurn thousands of years of accumulated tradition in favor of a text that gave them a direct and personal connection with God.

A Puritan had no use for the Church of England's Book of Common Prayer, since it tampered with the original meaning of the Bible and inhibited the spontaneity that they felt was essential to attaining a true and honest glimpse of the divine. Hymns were also judged to be a corruption of God's word—instead, a Puritan read directly from the Bible and sang scrupulously translated psalms whose meaning took precedence over the demands of rhyme and meter. As staunch "primitivists," Puritans refused to kneel while taking communion, since there was no evidence the apostles had done so during the Last Supper. There was also no biblical precedent for making the sign of the cross when uttering Christ's name. Even more important, there was no precedent for the system of bishops that ran the Church of England. The only biblically sanctioned organizational unit was the individual congregation.

Whatever deficiencies there may have been in Puritans' efforts to restore the teachings and practices of Christ's glorious church, no one can deny their passion as they sought to accomplish this goal. They spoke out against tradition. They defied authoritarian edicts that ran counter to the principles of church restoration. They sacrificed comfort and fortune to be obedient to God's calling. Many encountered torture, while others paid the ultimate price, being martyred for their faith. Their contribution to restoring New Testament Christianity must not be brushed aside lightly. They, as with other restorers in their own time and place, were heroes of the Christian faith.

8

Denominations Thrive in North America

1620 - 1800

The North American colonies offered new opportunities and fresh challenges for the glorious church. From the early days when the Pilgrims founded colonies along the New England Seaboard until the Revolutionary War concluded near the end of the eighteenth century, Christians in the New World were somewhat free to worship in accordance with their own beliefs. "Religious liberty" was a common refrain among immigrants who had crossed the Atlantic Ocean in search of greater personal freedoms. Many eschewed the heavy-handed practices of European churches, whether they were based in Rome, Canterbury, or Geneva.

Freedom of religion became inexorably linked to the colonial democratic lifestyle. There was no "Church of America"; each colony was free to establish its own laws regarding ecclesiastical orders and religious expression.

By choice, most of the colonies embraced the church as part of their political and social order. An "established church" was one that enjoyed favor of the government and was supported to some extent by taxes that were levied on its behalf. The earliest record of the church being treated with such favor was in the fourth century when Emperor Constantine legalized the church and made it an arm of the Roman Empire. A half century later, Emperor Theodosius recognized Christianity as the official religion of the Roman Empire. From that time forward, various nations laid claim to the church, establishing it in one form or another as its official religious body. A majority of the American colonies also chose to operate in this fashion.

Being more sympathetic to the practices of the Church of England than were their northern neighbors, southern colonies replicated the doctrines and worship rituals of the Anglican Church and acknowledged the church as an integral part of their social orders. After the War for Independence, the colonial Anglican Church was "Americanized," becoming known in most regions of North America as the Episcopal Church.

The Puritans, both those who had tried to purify the Church of England and those who preferred to separate from the state-controlled church, settled primarily in New England. These colonies also incorporated the church into their social orders, using local government to punish dissidents and discourage other sects from settling within their borders. But by the early eighteenth century, denominational churches were allowed to exist within the New England colonies, albeit holding no more than second-class status.

Under the strong influence of its founder, Lord Baltimore, Maryland was initially sympathetic to members of the Roman Catholic Church. It became a haven for those who had been in conflict with various forms of Protestantism. The Catholic sanctuary was short-lived, however, as Puritans were eventually allowed to move into Maryland, where they began to assert their separatist traditions. By the late seventeenth century, Catholicism was banned from the colony.

The Quakers, a congregational movement led by George Fox (1624 – 1691) and other dissidents who were opposed to the corruption that existed within the Church of England, migrated to North America, where they settled in Rhode Island and Pennsylvania. Laws pertaining to religion were more tolerant in Pennsylvania. Christian settlers who could not abide New England Puritanism and its punitive enforcement of a strict religious code of conduct often found refuge in the "Quaker Colony."

Adherents to the Quaker movement saw themselves as restorers, bringing back the rudimentary teaching of the early church after years of its apostasy. Central to their belief was "the priesthood of all believers," a doctrine that flew in the face of the Church of England and other highly structured bodies that relied heavily upon ordained clerics. The Quakers eschewed formal creeds and placed a high priority on piety and individual Bible study.

The frontier that lay west of the Appalachian Mountains and east of the Mississippi River was evangelized by circuit-riding ministers from various denominations, but none more than the Methodist preachers who followed a path set forth by John Wesley (1703 – 1791), his brother Charles Wesley (1707 – 1788), and their mutual friend George Whitefield (1714 – 1770). Although John Wesley always thought his religious teaching and practices lay within the tenets of the Anglican Church, Wesleyans were eventually determined to be a separate denomination. John Wesley did not embrace the Calvinist belief of predestination, calling upon his followers to press toward Christian maturity, taking methodical steps to become more like the disciples Jesus and his apostles taught them to be. Whitefield held to the more traditional view of Calvinism as adopted by the Anglican Church.

These were only a few of the many "brands" of Christianity that flourished in the colonies. Lutherans, Baptists, German Reformed, Presbyterians, and various denominations growing out of the Anabaptist movement also prospered under religious freedom. If colonial Christians weren't satisfied with their choices of a church body in their immediate community, they could start their own—and many did.

Over the passing of a hundred years of colonization, independent religious fervor began to thrive in the colonies. Without the strong presence of a pope and his henchmen, and without inquisitions that enforced the rulings of councils and synods, Christians enjoyed greater freedom to interpret the Scripture for themselves. It was part of the cherished lifestyle that was so popular an ocean away from the state-churches operating in the Old World.

But changes for the good are often counterbalanced by new practices that are flawed in other ways. The rigidity of European state-churches, with hierarchies of leadership and formal creeds that provided unity and structure for the believers, was replaced by an army of gifted preachers, persuasive in speech and capable of swaying large audiences to their own personal view of biblical thought. Instead of one glorious body of believers, the church became splintered into scores of denominations and lesser sects.

The emergence of denominationalism brought a fresh challenge to those who sought to restore the glory and simplicity of the early church. Rather than focusing upon a single church body, as did Martin Luther when he addressed the failings of the Roman Catholic Church, restorers in the colonies were forced to look in many directions all at once. Doctrine and religious practices were all over the map, and the most glaring corruption of the church had become its disunity; it was no longer a unified, single body as Jesus had prayed for it to be. Instead, it had evolved into a hodgepodge of factions, each preaching its rivals to hell.

Jonathan Edwards (1703 – 1758), a Yale graduate and a young preacher who had grown up under the Puritan influence in New England, and George Whitefield became the talk of the North American colonies in the 1730s and early 1740s. Both were talented speakers, capable of engaging large audiences with inspiring sermons, teaching both the goodness and severity of an eternal God.

Primarily Calvinist theologians, Edwards and Whitefield drew people from various Christian denominations to rousing revival meetings. Their preaching was not focused upon reform and restoration but was more of an ecumenical effort to bring sinners face-to-face with the call of God's saving grace. The movement, inspired by their zealous preaching, became known as "the Great Awakening," the first of several eras in which religious fervor spread through North America like a prairie fire.

The next generation of preachers drew upon the success of Whitefield and Edwards, but a few of them sought to address the denominational issue that had sorely divided the body of Christ. They wanted to shed sectarian "labels," calling all believers to come together as a united church in Christ. The seeds of restoration began to stir.

James O'Kelly (1735 – 1826) was a Methodist circuit rider, working primarily in North Carolina and Virginia. Having grown dissatisfied with the Methodist Church's practice of forcing ministerial appointments upon their preachers, O'Kelly filed a formal protest at a church conference in 1792. When his resolution did not prevail, he chose to break with the established Methodist Church, forming a new body designated as the Republican Methodist Church. The stated objective of the new church was to have no creed but the Bible. In 1801, the church abandoned its denominational name, and its members were known simply as "Christians."

Similarly, Abner Jones (1772 – 1841), a physician from New England, joined with another physician and preacher in the Baptist fellowship, Elias Smith (1769 – 1846), to form congregations that were not designated by denominational names. They abandoned human creeds, and their members were also known by no other name than Christians. These independent efforts to restore New Testament Christianity came about at the onset of the Second Great Awakening (circa 1800 – 1840), paving the way for three of the most effective church restorers of the nineteenth century, Thomas Campbell, his son Alexander Campbell, and Barton W. Stone.

9

An American Restoration Movement

1800 - 1832

Barton W. Stone (1772 – 1844)

Born in Maryland and raised by his widowed Episcopalian mother in Virginia, a youthful Barton W. Stone struggled with his decision to pursue a professional career in law or ministry. Unlike his contemporaries, who had experienced a "call to preach," Stone had not felt any such inner stirring. He determined initially, therefore, to study law.

It was after hearing James McGready (1760 – 1817), an itinerant Presbyterian minister, preach a series of sermons on "the Love of God" that Stone cast aside his plans to enter the legal profession and opted to devote himself to ministerial studies. A bright student, he explored biblical exegeses from many denominational sources, including the sermons he had heard from itinerant Methodist, Baptist, and Presbyterian preachers. He was ordained a Presbyterian minister in 1798 and began serving two small congregations in Kentucky, including the church at Cane Ridge.

Because his heart was open to the truth of God's will, regardless of the messenger, Stone soon found himself questioning major tenets of traditional Presbyterian doctrine. Calvinism, with its emphasis on predestination, left him with more questions than answers regarding a believer's hope for salvation. He also struggled with the apathetical approach to discipleship practiced by many of his parishioners. The young minister began to look for a more effective way to reach his flock.

Stone learned of nearby revival meetings where hundreds of nonbelievers became Christians after listening to compelling gospel preachers, so he made a trip to southern Kentucky, where he witnessed these evangelistic gatherings for himself. Armed with fresh ideas and a more emotional approach to his preaching, Stone purposed to host a revival in his own community.

In 1801, a six-day camp meeting was held in Cane Ridge, Kentucky, attracting an audience that was estimated by some to approach 30,000. Speakers included clerics from the Presbyterian Church, but Methodist and Baptist evangelists also participated in the historic event. The unified message focused upon "faith and repentance," with the hope of salvation being offered to "whosoever will."

The Presbyterian Synod of Kentucky, the governing body in charge of the denomination's activity within the state, took strong exception both to the doctrinal message proclaimed at the encampment and to the non-Presbyterian preachers who delivered some of the lessons. Stone and others who had participated in the revivals were called before the Synod to answer for their actions. A handful of the respondents, including Stone, chose to leave the Kentucky Synod and begin an alliance of their own—the Springfield Presbytery.

The newly formed organization lasted only a few months, however, before being dissolved. Its founders came to believe that there was no biblical basis for operating such a body. Stone, in his famous treatise entitled "Last Will and Testament of the Springfield Presbytery" (1804), broke ties with denominationalism, choosing to wear no other name than "Christian."

The Last Will and Testament of the Springfield Presbytery

1. "...there is but one body and one spirit, even as we are called in one hope of our calling.
2. "...our name of distinction, with its Reverend title, be forgotten..."
3. "...that our power for making laws for the government of the Church...forever cease;"
4. "...candidates for the gospel ministry...obtain license from God to preach the simple Gospel..."
5. "...that the Church of Christ resume her native right of internal government..."
6' "...that each particular church as a body...choose her own preacher and support him by a free-will offering..."
7. "...that the people henceforth take the Bible as the only sure guide to heaven..."
8. "...that preachers and people cultivate a spirit of mutual forbearance; pray more and dispute less..."

A dozen or more congregations in Kentucky and Ohio comprised the initial supporters in a movement that took root, calling upon Christians to abandon creeds and human traditions, returning to the Scripture as the ultimate authority for their faith. Most of the newly formed congregations became known as "Christian churches" or "churches of Christ," similar to those spawned a decade earlier by James O'Kelly, Abner Jones, and Elias Smith.

Thomas Campbell (1763 – 1854)
Alexander Campbell (1788 – 1866)

Church restoration's most energetic era occurred in the United States during the first half of the nineteenth century. This initiative grew partially out of a contemporary movement in Scotland, where a band of restorers led by John Glas, Robert Sandeman, Greville Ewing, James Haldane, and his brother Robert Haldane found common cause in calling Christians to return to the simplicity of the New Testament church. Rejecting the church-state ties of the Church of Scotland, these educated men urged all who would listen to follow the Scripture and to operate local congregations without allegiance to any state-sponsored church body.

Among those influenced by these restoration-minded Scots was Alexander Campbell, a bright young man who aspired to become a Presbyterian minister. Spending a year in Glasgow before joining his father in the United States, Alexander listened carefully to the neo-Congregationalists and discovered that much of their teaching was in harmony with his understanding of the New Testament. Alexander found himself less enamored with a state-church model. Although he did not publicly renounce his Presbyterian heritage while in Scotland, he had decided in his heart that he could no longer abide the authoritarian practices of his heritage and refused to participate in the Seceder communion services. By the time he reached the New World in 1809 and was united with his father, he was open to a new way of thinking about his church affiliation, and so was his father, Thomas Campbell, an Irish Presbyterian minister who had immigrated to America in 1807.

Prior to his son's arrival in the States, Thomas Campbell had been censored by his own brethren for being too tolerant of Christians outside his Seceder Presbyterian fellowship. Rather than capitulate to the discipline imposed upon him, Campbell took a step in the other direction. He established a Bible study group and articulated its purposes in a treatise entitled the "Declaration and Address." This document, written in 1809, called for Christians from all denominations to unite, casting aside their human creeds and finding common footing in the Scripture alone. Campbell's intent was not to found a new denomination but to bring about Christian unity with less regard for sectarian branding.

Declaration and Address

From the introduction: "Our desire...would be that, rejecting human opinions and the inventions of men as of any authority...we might forever cease from further contentions...taking the divine Word alone for our rule..."

1. "That the Church of Christ upon earth is essentially, intentionally and constitutionally one..."

2. "That although the Church of Christ upon earth must necessarily exist...locally separate one from another, yet there ought to be no...divisions among them..."

3. "That...nothing ought to be inculcated upon Christians... but what is expressly taught and enjoined upon them in the Word of God."

4. "That...the New Testament is as perfect a constitution for the worship, discipline, and government of the New Testament Church..."

5. "Nothing ought to be received into the faith or worship of the Church, or be made a term of communion among Christians, that is not as old as the New Testament."

6. "...no such deductions or inferential truth ought to have any place in the Church's confession."

7. "That although doctrinal exhibitions...be highly expedient... they ought not to be made terms of Christian communion..."

8. "...self-knowledge respecting [one's] lost and perishing condition...and of the way of salvation through Jesus Christ, accompanied with a profession of their faith in the obedience to him, in all things, according to his Word, is all that is absolutely necessary to qualify them for admission into his Church."

9. "That all who are able through grace to make such a profession...should consider each other the precious saints of God, should love each other as brethren...members of the same body..."

10. "That divisions among the Christians is a horrid evil, fraught with many evils..."

11. "That...neglect of the expressly revealed will of God...and... making...human opinions...a term of communion...are... causes of all corruptions and divisions that ever have taken place in the Church of God."

12. "...that in all their administrations they keep close by the observance of all divine ordinances, after the example of the primitive Church, exhibited in the New Testament, without any additions whatever of human opinions or inventions of men."

13. "Lastly, that if any circumstantials indispensably necessary to the observance of divine ordinances be not found upon the pages of expressed revelation, such...should be adopted under the title of human expedients [but]...the observance of these things might produce no contention or division in the Church."

As Thomas Campbell's writings became known, his relationship with the Presbyterian Church grew more tenuous. He was denied the opportunity to serve as a minister, his doctrinal positions being far too ecumenical to be accepted by the church fathers of his day. In 1812, demonstrating a mutual respect for the inviolate truth of the Scripture, Thomas and Alexander Campbell, along with their wives, were baptized, being fully immersed in the waters of Buffalo Creek by Matthias Luce, a Baptist minister.

A year later, the Brush Run Church, which Alexander Campbell helped organize in 1811, became affiliated with the Redstone Baptist Association. The younger Campbell distinguished himself both as a gifted writer and as a renowned debater of church doctrine. He wrote and circulated the "Christian Baptist," a publication that added stature to his emerging reputation as a stalwart church restorer.

Alexander Campbell never intended for his association with the Baptists to be anything more than a place to enjoy fellowship while he continued his quest to bring Christians from all denominations into the larger fellowship of Christ's church. It was a place to park, a place from which his plea for nonsectarian Christianity could be heard. Throughout these years within the Baptist fellowship, Campbell planted a number of independent churches, each operating as an autonomous body.

It was not until 1824 that Barton Stone and Alexander Campbell met for the first time. Both men had enjoyed considerable success in their respective ministerial careers, calling upon Christians to take a Bible-centered approach to faith and fellowship; but their paths had not crossed until Campbell made an evangelistic tour through Kentucky and paid a visit to Stone, a fellow church restorer.

The two men were not cut of the same cloth. Campbell was the orator, the debater, and a man who took hardline positions on doctrinal issues, while Stone was more professorial, a man of grace, and one who sought to be inclusive in his work among Christians of every denomination. Campbell preferred to use the name "disciples" to describe baptized believers, whereas Stone used the name "Christians." Stone believed in a more personal influence of the Holy Spirit in the lives of Christians; Campbell held to the position that the work of the Holy Spirit was through the reading of God's Holy Word.

What Stone and Campbell held in common, however, was much stronger than their differences in style and personality. Within a few years of their initial meeting in Kentucky, Campbell began to distance himself from the Baptist Church, pursuing a course more like the independent approach launched by Stone a decade earlier. In January 1832, following an extended meeting of the principals and some of their congregants who had gathered in Lexington, Kentucky, the two movements merged.

The task of blending two groups comprised of autonomous congregations, neither with a national organization to speak authoritatively for its collective fellowship, was not easy. Emissaries from both sides travelled among the existing congregations, urging them to consolidate where possible and calling on believers from all denominations to discard their allegiance to human creeds. The overriding objective was to unite Christians into one spiritual body that belonged to Jesus Christ. What resulted was a passionate approach to evangelism that exploded throughout the greater Ohio Valley.

From the time of the Stone-Campbell merger and going forward, Alexander Campbell became a formidable personality in American history. Through his writings, his preaching, and some of his widely publicized debates, Campbell was known among people of faith and among many secular leaders as well. James Madison, fourth president of the United States, once said of Campbell, "I regard him as the ablest and most original expounder of the Scriptures I have ever heard."

10

Restoration Becomes the Rage

1832 - 1865

Before the first shots were fired in America's Civil War (1861), significant growth occurred in the ranks of those who were part of a regional religious revival, commonly known as the Restoration Movement. The combined efforts of Barton Stone and Alexander Campbell, along with a cadre of zealous evangelists, created a groundswell of conversions and resulted in an eightfold increase in membership among the independent Christian churches—from 25,000 adherents to more than 200,000. The first half of the nineteenth century was, as some have described it, the "golden age of church restoration."

The movement's widespread appeal was attributable to several key factors. First, the message for Christians to rid themselves of human creeds resonated with those who were tired of heavy-handed clerics, brow-beating parishioners with long lists of "dos" and "don'ts." Thomas Campbell's call to "speak where the Bible speaks and be silent where it is silent" (Declaration and Address) made perfect sense.

Second, the overriding theme of these restorers was to "unite" Christians rather than having them divided into scores of branded sects and denominations. Over a period of three hundred years, the Christian church, once a single body, had transformed into a mishmash of churches, each claiming the purest dogma and often condemning its rivals to the deepest recesses of hell. The idea of Christians coming from many different backgrounds, being united in a single church and drawn together in fellowship by their common love of the Lord, was a refreshing refrain.

Perhaps the strongest appeal was the simplicity of the movement's message. Walter Scott (1796 – 1861), an immigrant from Scotland and a colleague of Alexander Campbell, was an exceptionally gifted evangelist. When those who attended his revival meetings sought answers to questions about "salvation," Scott made a clear call to the lost, urging them to repent of their transgressions, believe in the lordship of Jesus Christ, and be baptized for the remission of their sins. They responded by the thousands.

Word of Walter Scott's successful campaigns soon reached the ears of Alexander Campbell. Fearing that the large responses to his friend's preaching may have been borne of some wayward teaching, Campbell asked his father, Thomas Campbell, to visit Scott and to listen to him preach at one or more of the meetings. Shortly thereafter, the elder Campbell sent a letter to his son, reassuring him that Scott's message was sound and that he had personally witnessed the "restoration plea" being proclaimed in the field with unprecedented results. The movement gained its footing as preachers from sectarian churches began preaching a more nondenominational approach to Christian fellowship.

The movement was also fueled by the uncommon success that Alexander Campbell enjoyed as a participant in a series of formal debates. He won favor among all Christians, regardless of their denominational affiliation, when he debated agnostics who were skeptical about the existence of God; he was a champion of all Protestants when debating key issues with members of the Roman Catholic Church; and he set the table for Walter Scott and other evangelists when he challenged the biblical authority for Calvinism, insisting that adult baptism by immersion was what penitent believers must do in order to receive God's gift of salvation that had been offered through Calvary's cross.

The transcripts of these debates were distributed widely and read with keen interest. Campbell and his evangelistic colleagues were making the case for all Christians to unite in one body, using the Scripture as their guide. In an era when secular distractions and entertainment opportunities were few, conversation about the circuit riders and their gospel call to repentance was popular both in the cities and in rural America. The Restoration Movement flourished in the midst of an historic spiritual awakening that was spreading rapidly throughout the nation's western frontier.

Although a measure of unity existed among the restoration-minded congregations, they were by no means identical in faith and practice. Alexander Campbell and Barton Stone themselves didn't agree on every interpretation of biblical text, and they didn't expect their followers to agree on every point of doctrine in order to enjoy fellowship with one another. Stone allowed for much greater intervention of the Holy Spirit in the everyday lives of Christians than Campbell was comfortable to acknowledge. The Campbells pressed for an adherence to essential tenets of faith in order to achieve unity, while Stone opened the lines of fellowship, even to the point of including adults who had not been immersed.

The diversity among the movement's congregations was fueled in part by the Christian periodicals, written by editors representing many differing points of view in this loosely knit affiliation of believers. Until his death in 1844, Stone edited *The Christian Messenger*. "Let the unity of Christians be our polar star" was the journal's constant theme. After Alexander Campbell severed his ties with the Baptist Church and stopped his writings for the *Christian Baptist*, he launched a new publication, the *Millennial Harbinger,* which he edited from 1830 until his death in 1866. Tolbert Fanning founded a new publication, the *Gospel Advocate* (1855), which became the voice for the restoration plea in the South.

At some point it became obvious to leaders of the movement that the only way to sustain the momentum that had been achieved over a decade or two was to establish colleges that were led by Christians who were receptive of the restoration plea. These institutions of higher learning were equipped to educate the next generation of gospel preachers and to saturate them with the message of unity in one body belonging to Jesus Christ. In 1836, Walter Scott became the first president of Bacon College in Georgetown, Kentucky, and Alexander Campbell founded his own institution, Bethany College, in West Virginia in 1840. These colleges, and more of them that followed, graduated many of the leaders who perpetuated the restoration plea for the remainder of the century.

If this account were a fairy tale, it would conclude with all Christians denouncing their denominational ties, uniting in one glorious church body, and living happily ever after. We could only wish it had been that easy. Great strides were made under the leadership of the Campbells and Stone, but a nation divided over social and economic issues brought new challenges to the Restoration Movement. The goal of bringing Christians together with a nondenominational approach still had appeal, but a "War Between the States" was at the forefront of everyone's mind. The deaths of Stone (1844), Thomas Campbell (1854), and Alexander Campbell (1866), along with a four-year civil war, sucked the wind out of the movement for a season. It remained to be seen in what direction the church would move after the peace agreement at Appomattox.

11

Walls within the Movement

1866 - 1906

The extraordinary leadership of Barton Stone, Thomas and Alexander Campbell, Walter Scott, and men of their ilk was a significant factor in promoting church restoration during the first half of the nineteenth century. Their evangelistic sermons, extensive writings, and persuasive skills in formal debates also left a blueprint for future generations to follow.

When new converts struggled to recall Scripture to support their faith, they still remembered the restorers' familiar slogans. If asked about doctrine, they might respond, "We speak where the Bible speaks and we remain silent where the Bible is silent," or simply, "We have no creed but Christ." When referring to the rapidly growing body of believers, they might describe themselves by using the refrain, "We may not be the only Christians, but we are 'Christians' only." Catch phrases were useful in uniting a fellowship that had no authoritative hierarchy. These independent Christians were on a mission to unite all believers into one church body that adhered to the original teaching and practices of the nondenominational apostolic church.

At the commencement of America's Civil War, a survey of restoration-minded Christians accounted for approximately 1,200 congregations in the North and 800 in the South. Four years later, the scars from four years of fierce fighting had intensified regional differences, and conditions were ripe for the movement to splinter.

The establishment of the American Christian Missionary Society, designed to oversee worldwide evangelism, became a lightning rod for debate. Alexander Campbell was favorable to its founding in 1849 and was named the society's first president. Dissenters argued that mission efforts were the work of the local church, not something that could be delegated to an auxiliary body. Following the war, churches in the South deepened their disapproval of any missionary society. David Lipscomb, who had succeeded Tolbert Fanning as editor of the *Gospel Advocate* in Nashville, allowed no quarter for any organization that threatened to usurp authority reserved to the local congregations.

The Christian Standard, a weekly publication founded in Cincinnati after the war, was more favorable to the existence of missionary societies. Isaac Errett, the paper's first editor, fought for a more "progressive church" that was in keeping with the culture of a post-war era. For two decades, Errett and Lipscomb clashed in their editorials, waging a war of words that opened a wider chasm between the churches of the North and the South. Many of the editorials focused directly on the causes and outcomes of the recent "War Between the States," making it harder for old wounds to heal.

Making existing difficulties worse, another issue of disagreement arose. It focused on the question of whether congregations affiliated with the Restoration Movement would use instrumental music in corporate worship assemblies. The matter had not been a point of great concern prior to the Civil War. In trying to restore New Testament church practices, leaders of the movement generally agreed that what the apostolic church did with music would set the bar for the church in the nineteenth century. Since instruments of music were not introduced into the church's public assembly until hundreds of years after Peter's sermon on Pentecost, hardly any of the leaders proposed that it be used in the contemporary congregations.

But in 1860, a year before the war commenced, the church in Midway, Kentucky, incorporated a melodeon into the worship as a means of supporting its ineffectual song service. Editors of the Christian journals came out of their skins. Those in the North found a new issue to debate, while editors in the South took less time to write about the topic because congregations in their region almost universally rejected the use of instruments of music.

The crisis was not the first time the church had struggled with the issue of music. Opposition to mechanical instruments occurred in the Roman Church in the seventh century when first introduced into the public mass. The Great Schism of 1054, dividing the Western Church of Rome from the Eastern Church in Constantinople, raised the issue once again. Orthodox churches in the East vehemently opposed using the instrument, as most of them do today. In the early sixteenth century, two of the early church reformers, Huldreich Zwingli and John Calvin, called for the abolition of mechanical instruments in worship. Now, at another time and place, Restoration Movement congregations fought a battle that had gone unresolved for centuries.

In 1872, when the Central Christian Church in Cincinnati opened its new 2,000-seat assembly hall, complete with its $8,000 organ, the gloves came off. Over the next three decades a growing schism erupted between a generally well-financed church in parts of the North and its less affluent kinsmen in the South. The result was a split in a movement whose main objective was to unify Christians as one body of believers.

Although the missionary society and instrumental music were the issues that generated the most ink in Christian periodicals of that day, other factors were also at play in creating tension among the congregations. Prior to the war, differences on the existence of a missionary society could be expressed without giving thought to dividing the fellowship. Bad feelings caused by the federal government's Reconstruction Program in the South magnified the differences between the two regions, turning small squabbles into a lingering feud.

In 1906, when the United States Census Bureau published its national report on church membership, a line of demarcation was drawn between Disciples Churches and Christian Churches principally in northern states and Churches of Christ mainly in the South. By far, the Disciples/Christian Church was larger, with 8,293 congregations boasting 982,701 members, compared to 2,649 congregations of the Churches of Christ and only 159,658 members. Fractures within the Restoration Movement, previously known primarily within the fellowship, were now made public.

The dream of uniting Christians into one glorious church experienced a setback with the publication of the census, but the fervor of the restoration plea and the principles associated with the movement lived on. Many Christians in the South deemed their northern brethren to have capitulated to the culture that looked unfavorably upon a loosely affiliated body of autonomous congregations as "not being a *proper church*." To southerners, the Disciples' insistence on approving the instrument and missionary societies was perceived as evidence that these congregations in the North had become a denomination, fashioning their fellowship after the wishes of men rather than following apostolic example.

The Churches of Christ in the South intensified their efforts to advance the restoration message, but northern churches characterized southern doctrine as being narrow-minded, not fitting in with the times, and appearing to be nothing more than a sect. The glorious church of Jesus Christ had much to overcome as it plunged headlong into the twentieth century.

12

Restoration Plea Envelops the Globe

1906 - 2000

When Jesus proclaimed, "I will build my church and the Gates of Hades shall not prevail against it" (Matthew 16:18), none of his disciples had in mind that this invincible body would become a regionalized church located in an unknown country located halfway around the world. The church was always intended to be a worldwide fellowship of all men and women who had surrendered to Jesus Christ as their Lord and Master. It was to be a universal body.

It is not surprising to learn that the Roman Catholic Church had sent missionaries across the globe for centuries. These brave harbingers of God's love paid the same price the apostles did as they sought to work with people who viewed them with skepticism and contempt. Many were persecuted and martyred for their faith.

As Protestant denominations emerged following the Reformation in the sixteenth century, they also became mission-minded, sending brave clerics into new lands being opened to exploration and colonization. The Bible was being taught among people who had never heard the name of Jesus, and some opened their hearts to Christianity. The Lord was "adding to the church daily those who were being saved" (Acts 2:47).

At the turn of the twentieth century, Christians affiliated with the Restoration Movement were well-intended in their efforts to restore the apostolic church in every conceivable way: how it was organized, how it used biblical terminology to describe and to define itself, how it worshipped, how it practiced fellowship, and how it engaged in local and international evangelism. Injured by their recent split with congregations in the North, the nondenominational Churches of Christ redoubled their efforts to become champions of the restoration plea. Being true to that standard included doing what was needed to fulfill the Great Commission: taking the gospel into the entire world, "making disciples of all the nations" (Matt. 28:19).

Without a national organization or a missionary society to organize foreign evangelism, the local congregations were not well equipped for the task. Furthermore, most of the viable Christian colleges affiliated with the Restoration Movement were in the North and aligned with the Disciples or conservative Christian Church congregations. Two notable exceptions were David Lipscomb College and Freed-Hardeman College, located in Tennessee, each of which had roots in prior institutions that existed before the turn of the century.

Leaders of the Churches of Christ began the daunting task of building "structure" within their fellowship in order to survive. Abilene Christian College was founded on the West Texas prairie in 1906, Harding College began in Arkansas in 1924, and Pepperdine College opened in Los Angeles in 1937. These institutions of higher learning were not under the direct oversight of the churches, but their trustees, administrators, and faculty shared the restoration heritage. Many preachers, missionaries, elders, deacons, Bible school teachers, social workers, and parents of Christ-centered homes received a "Christian education," flavored in great measure by the principles of the Restoration Movement.

From these colleges, young men and women, motivated to fulfill the Great Commission, committed themselves to Christian service in all parts of the world. They spent years of their lives teaching and preaching in China, India, Africa, Europe, and

Latin America. They founded schools, opened orphanages, and provided medical services in the name of the Lord Jesus Christ. These zealots took with them the gospel in its simplest form, as it had been handed down by Walter Scott and other forbearers, and they sought to plant nondenominational congregations wherever they went. The Restoration Movement became a global effort, expanding the church in non-Christian countries, while fortifying its base back in the States.

The Churches of Christ experienced unparalleled growth in the first half of the twentieth century. Evangelists were focused on a mission to "save the lost," and they did so by conducting debates with denominational preachers, holding gospel meetings in the local church buildings, or brush arbor revivals in rural parts of the country. From a collective membership of 159,658 as calculated in the 1906 religious census, these independent churches grew to somewhere close to 2.5 million by the late 1960s. In 1967, United Press International proclaimed that Churches of Christ were the "fastest-growing major church body in the United States." The data supporting that claim has come under criticism in more recent years for not being based on substantiated information, but the fact remains that church growth was occurring during this era at an unparalleled pace.

As this fellowship of churches became more prominent in American culture, the attending growth of quasi-church organizations also became more apparent. Congregations began to build more impressive church buildings that helped broaden their appeal to higher socioeconomic strata. More colleges, children's homes, and social outreach organizations were established both for their own intrinsic value and as a means to provide further support for congregations that were advancing the restoration plea.

Impressive growth, however, came with a price. Factions crept into the homogeneous fellowship, causing fissures over a variety of issues: whether it was scriptural to have Sunday Bible classes at the church buildings; whether there should be one cup or multiple cups in the observance of the Lord's Supper; whether church buildings should have kitchens; whether children's homes should be supported with funds from the congregation's treasury; and a host of other issues that lent themselves to debilitating debate.

While the rhetoric of the fellowship continued to espouse the restoration plea, the reality was something less than a united front. In some of the churches, legalism replaced the Stone-Campbell call for Christians to unite in one body. Defensive responses to any form of progressive thought built walls around the church, isolating it from denominationalism but creating the appearance of churches becoming a narrow-minded sect.

Meanwhile, the Restoration Movement's northern churches were having problems of their own. Soon after the census of 1906, a liberal-conservative break separated the Disciples (liberal) from the Christian Church (conservative). These two factions, plus the Churches of Christ in the South, left three distinct fellowships emanating from the Stone-Campbell movement that had begun a century ago.

In the passing of a few decades, the Disciples of Christ evolved into a self-acknowledged denomination, eventually renouncing its support of the restoration plea. The independent Christian churches operated more akin to their southern cousins, adhering to conservative doctrines on most issues—the notable exception being their acceptance of instrumental music in the public worship. Whereas the Disciples experienced a steady decline in numbers throughout the latter part of the twentieth century, Christian churches tapped into the popularity of community churches and independent Bible churches, enjoying renewed growth in many states across the nation.

13

God's Glorious Church in the 21st Century

2001 - Present

Preaching at the Mayfair Church of Christ in Oklahoma City, M. Norvel Young, a minister and Christian educator of the twentieth century, made this observation about the process of restoring the church: "Restoration is *not* like the unveiling of a statue in the park; an event that occurs but once, allowing the sculpture to stand thereafter unattended for the ages." Young went on to say, "Restoration is a calling that belongs to each generation."

It remains to be seen what the Churches of Christ will do with the challenge of restoration in the twenty-first century. On one hand, restoring the church is, after all, a work of the Lord, not merely an exercise of man. Indeed, God uses the talents of men and women to complete his will, but without his blessings, efforts to restore the apostolic church in any generation would be futile. Before anything else, it would behoove the church to petition the Lord to bless its best efforts, whatever they may be, and to keep his presence ever before them.

Of some concern in this matter of restoration is the overall direction of church leadership today. Have the Churches of Christ become a denomination? That would not have been anyone's intention, but the isolationist policies of the church in recent decades and an acrimonious defense of traditional church practices have led some to believe the Restoration Movement has run aground. They fear that the plea of uniting Christians in one body has resulted in the branding of a fellowship that will allow itself to be known exclusively by a singular name—the "Churches of Christ."

Supporting that point of view is the common usage of the term "Church of Christ" as an adjective: *Church of Christ schools*, or *Church of Christ journals*, or *Church of Christ children's homes*. This practice forces the question: to whom do these entities belong? Do they belong to the church? Does the Lord's glorious church have a "branded name," all others being anathema to its founder? Could New Testament Christians worship in a building that didn't have "Church of Christ" emblazoned on the wall or on an electronic sign on the front lawn? There is a case to be made that among a segment of the membership, the Churches of Christ have become what its members abhor the most—a sect or another denomination.

Equally dangerous is a course that too many leaders appear to be taking. Fearful of being out of touch with the times, some congregations have moved more in the direction of their cousins, the Disciples of Christ, abandoning the restoration plea because it grates against the culture. It's not "politically correct." It's not "user friendly." Its marketing approach is totally out of sync with the "unchurched" masses. No one wants to hear sermons about "heaven" or "hell" anymore.

You want to introduce the instrument into public worship even though the apostolic church and the church for hundreds of years thereafter deliberately chose not to incorporate it into the assembly? Sure, why not.

You want women to preach and lead the church as elders of the flock? No problem.

The solution for these progressives is to take no firm stands, allowing people to believe as they will and holding to few doctrinal restraints. This practice also leads to denominationalism, or worse—the church's becoming nothing more than a social organization that parallels the work of government and private agencies. A *church* may remain, but it has lost its *glory*. It no longer exists as a unique body whose mission is to seek the lost and bring them to the Lord.

To restore the Lord's glorious church in the twenty-first century will require strong leadership, much as it has in centuries past. It will require Christians to become more knowledgeable of God's will as revealed in the Bible and to make Scripture, once again, the authoritative guide in church governance. It will require a fellowship of believers to dedicate themselves to the call of reaching lost souls with the gospel message, while leaving the matter of salvation itself to the Lord. The thought of being "Christians only" without having to be the "only Christians" is a course that speaks of humility and grace, allowing God to be God and recognizing disciples as the sheep of his pasture—not the gatekeepers of God's heaven.

Restoration has never been an easy process. Ask Josiah or Hezekiah. Ask Paul, who wrote tirelessly to the early churches, trying to bring them back to the pure essence of what God would have them to be. Ask men of the Reformation Era, such as Martin Luther and Hulderich Zwingli, whose lives were threatened by their bold attempts to bring apostolic practices back to a church that had drifted away. Walk a mile in the shoes of Barton Stone or Thomas and Alexander Campbell as they began a prairie fire with their appeal to unite Christians into one nondenominational body. If restoration has a chance in the present generation, it will require exceptional leadership—leaders who love the Lord and believe in his promise to build one universal church.

Where does a fresh approach to restoration begin? In order to look forward, the church must look back. Back to its origin, back to the Scripture that defines its purpose, its function, its methods, and its message. It is not enough to restore the framework while leaving the spirit of the church unexamined. Love, humility, gracious behavior, courage, and forgiveness must be restored in the *bride* as they are exemplified in the *bridegroom*.

At the center of the church's message must be the theme that Paul preached to the Corinthians: "I determined not to know anything among you except Jesus Christ and him crucified" (1 Corinthians 2:2). He is the cog; the church is the wheel. Everything the church does must revolve around him. The church, after all, belongs to him. He made the ultimate sacrifice with his own blood to redeem the church. The church must never be placed on a pedestal that supersedes its founder.

Finally, the message of the church must be one that unites believers into one body. There was a time when the Churches of Christ were outspoken in their plea for nondenominational Christianity. "Neither Catholic, Protestant, nor Jew" was the mantra. That emphasis needs to find a new voice in the twenty-first century. In recent decades, the appeal for nondenominational Christianity has been taught more effectively by community churches and independent Bible churches. Churches of Christ, by whatever name, need to champion the theme that was at the heart of Jesus' prayer in John 17—that his disciples be one as the Father and the Son are one.

In that same prayer, Jesus went on to petition the Father with this thought: "And the *glory* which you gave me I have given them, that they may be one just as we are one" (John 17:22).

Paul spoke well when he described the Lord's love for his church:

"Husbands, love your wives just as Christ also loved the church and gave himself for her, that he might sanctify and cleanse her with the washing of water by the word, that he might present her to himself a glorious church, not having spot or wrinkle or any such thing, but that she should be holy and without blemish." (Ephesians 5:25-27)

May the Lord strengthen the resolve of Christians in the twenty-first century to restore the apostolic church to its intended place of honor, that it might become the glorious church he called it to be when he made it his bride.

A Glorious Church
Discussion Questions

Chapter 1
A Glorious Church – Holy and Without Blemish

1. How is the relationship of Christ and his church similar to the marriage relationship?

2. How would you describe the reputation of the church in contemporary American society?

3. If given the task to restore the church to its intended glory, what steps would you take to achieve the intended result?

4. Which New Testament church most resembles the congregation you attend?

5. What are some convincing arguments for believing that the Bible is the inspired word of God?

Chapter 2
The Post-Apostolic Church

1. Reflect upon the early church's structure, worship, and ministries. How do they differ from your experience with the church today?

2. How does persecution in the church manifest itself today? How should the church respond?

3. Were the controversies of the early church more foundational to faith than the controversies of today? Explain your answer.

4. In what ways did ecumenical councils and creeds preserve church unity, and in what ways did they open the door for division?

5. What caused the church to multiply so rapidly in the first century? What can be done to replicate this pace of growth today?

6. Before the New Testament canon was completed, what was the basis for determining proper church governance?

Chapter 3
The Events Leading to the Great Schism

1. From the time of Constantine, the state and the church have been somewhat interactive. How has this relationship aided the church, and how has it hindered the church?

2. What effect did the fall of the Roman Empire have on the development of the church?

3. Through the centuries, the church became more and more centralized in its structure. How did this shift impact the church?

4. What have been the long-term consequences of Muhammad's birth near the end of the sixth century?

5. Does government stability ensure church stability? Is it possible for political upheaval to help stabilize the church?

6. Which of the differences between Eastern Orthodox and Roman Catholic theology are the most critical? Can you identify any "restoration factor" amidst this schism?

Chapter 4
The Church Goes To War

1. Would you consider the Crusades a "just and holy war" against the influence of Islam? If so, would such an endeavor be considered just today?

2. Can people be converted through force and intimidation? How has the modern church used such tactics to persuade people to follow Jesus or to conform to a theological ideology?

3. When a church finds itself in a strong financial position, how can it protect itself from the pitfalls of wealth?

4. How do academic and scholastic pursuits aid the church? How can scholarship become a detriment to the church?

Chapter 5
The Groundwork for Reformation

1. How would you define the terms "reformer" and "restorer"?

2. Those that laid the groundwork for the Reformation, such as Waldo, Wycliffe, and Hus, were insistent on "laymen" preachers. What are the advantages and disadvantages of this idea?

3. Should the church only practice what is expressly authorized in text, like the Taborites, or should it accept any practice that is not expressly condemned, like the Ultraquists?

4. How has nationalism impacted the church's mission and ministry?

5. How do you differentiate works of merit from works of righteousness?

6. What justification, if any, could the church have for exacting corporal or capital punishment upon those deemed to be heretics?

Chapter 6
The Protestant Reformation

1. Martin Luther championed the idea of "a priesthood of believers." What does that phrase mean for the church today?

2. Zwingli pushed for the sermon to be "the primary event" in worship. Do you agree?

3. Do you ascribe to the teaching that proclaims the "presence of Christ" is in the Lord's Supper? If so, how is he present?

4. Though Luther, Zwingli, and Calvin shared a belief in the authority of Scripture, they were diverse in their application of the text. How would you explain this? Is there "room" for diversity of thought in the church?

5. How do you differentiate between church tradition and biblical tradition? How does tradition help the church, and how does it hurt the church?

6. What leadership skills did the reformers possess in common? What leadership skills are needed today to be effective in restoring the New Testament church?

Chapter 7
Reformation in England and Scotland

1. Queen Elizabeth I used government in an attempt to force church attendance. What tactics should church leaders use to encourage attendance at the weekly assembly?

2. Elizabeth's theology was deemed "a middle-of-the-road theology" between Catholicism and Protestantism. How prevalent is "middle-of-the-road theology" in today's church?

3. The Puritans had a noble vision for the church. Would you consider their effort a success or failure?

4. Is there a place for Puritanical zeal in today's church?

5. To what extent should the church employ resources like the *Book of Common Prayer* to aid in worship or spiritual disciplines?

6. What motivated King Henry VIII to separate the Church of England from the Roman Catholic Church? Do churches continue to split for frivolous reasons?

Chapter 8
Denominations Thrive in the Colonies

1. Was America founded as a Christian nation?

2. What are the positive and negative outflows of religious freedom?

3. How would you describe the ideal relationship between church and state?

4. How has freedom of religion impacted interpretation of biblical text?

5. The Great Awakening was propelled by powerful preaching that focused on the individual. How would you describe powerful preaching in today's church?

6. What is a denomination? How does it differ from a sect? What did Paul teach about sectarianism?

7. How much influence do preachers have in shaping the doctrinal positions of the church?

8. "What's in a name?" Does it matter that some believers choose to be known by denominational names?

Chapter 9
An American Restoration Movement

1. What is a creed? What are the benefits of exploring the teachings of all Christian traditions?

2. Which items in "The Last Will and Testament of the Springfield Presbytery" strike you as the most crucial to church restoration?

3. Read through Thomas Campbell's "Declaration and Address." Which items do you find the most compelling, especially in light of church practices today?

4. What can Christians learn from Alexander Campbell and Barton Stone putting aside their differences for the goal of church unity and restoration?

5. How can autonomous congregations remain united without compromising their core beliefs?

Chapter 10
Restoration Becomes the Rage

1. Was Alexander Campbell correct in questioning the teaching behind Walter Scott's successful work?

2. How can restoration occur when those who desire restoration disagree on how it should be achieved?

3. One historian noted that the Churches of Christ did not need bishops because they had editors. How have church publications aided in restoration, and how have they detracted from it?

4. What has been the role of Christian colleges within the Restoration Movement?

5. How do social and economic issues factor into the goal of restoration?

6. In what ways do public debates over church doctrine benefit or detract from the mission of the church?

Chapter 11
Walls Within the Movement

1. How do you interpret the following mantra of the early Restoration Movement: "Christians only, but not the only Christians"?

2. Do you see quasi-church organizations, such as the American Christian Missionary Society, as being beneficial to the ministry of the church? Why has its work been so controversial?

3. What are the most explosive issues in the church today? How can these issues be properly addressed in churches?

4. When is division necessary in order to maintain the goal of restoration?

5. What effect did the American Civil War have on the Restoration Movement?

6. When the Scripture is silent on an issue, does it require prohibition of that practice or allow license?

Chapter 12
Restoration Plea Envelops the Globe

1. What factors led to the rapid growth of the Churches of Christ in the early twentieth century?

2. How should we interrelate with churches that hold different views regarding whether to conduct Bible classes, support children's homes from the church treasury, or how to distribute the elements of the Lord's Supper?

3. What are the greatest obstacles to worldwide evangelism?

4. How can the church redirect its focus outward rather than inward?

5. What is your understanding of the terms "legalism," "liberalism," and "traditionalism" when applied to the church today?

6. What are some of the fundamental differences between the Churches of Christ, the Disciples of Christ, and the Independent Christian Church? What beliefs do these three fellowships hold in common?

Chapter 13
God's Glorious Church in the 21st Century

1. Assess the modern church's success in carrying out the restoration plea.

2. What can churches do to avoid falling into the traps of sectarianism?

3. How does the church today remain relevant while adhering to ancient principles and teaching?

4. How "glorious" is the New Testament Church in the twenty-first century?

A Glorious Church

Bibliography

General Historical Resources

Cairns, Earle, *Christianity Through the Centuries*. Grand Rapids: Zondervan Publishing House, 1981.

Ferguson, Everett, *Church History Volume 1*. Grand Rapids: Zondervan, 2005.

Livingstone, E. A., *Oxford Concise Dictionary of the Christian Church*. Oxford, England: Oxford University Press, 2000.

Scott, I. Julius, *Jewish Backgrounds of the New Testament*. Grand Rapids: Baker Books, 2000.

Smith, William, *Old Testament History* Joplin: College Press, 1973.

Walker, Williston, *A History of the Christian Church*. New York: Charles Scribner's Sons, 1959.

Woodbridge, John, and Frank James, *Church History Volume 2*. Grand Rapids: Zondervan, 2013.

Apostolic and Patristic Time Periods

Campbell, Ted A., *Christian Confessions*. Louisville: Westminster John Knox Press, 1996.

"Church Fathers," *Christian Classics Ethereal Library*. www.ccel.org.

Ferguson, Everett, *Baptism in the Early Church*. Grand Rapids: William B. Eardmans Publishing, 2009.

Reese, Gareth L., *New Testament History Acts*. Joplin: College Press, 1993.

Schaff, Philip, *The Creeds of Christendom 3 Volumes*. Grand Rapids: Baker Books, 1998.

Wogaman, J. Philip, and Douglas Strong, *Readings in Christian Ethics*, Louisville: Westminster John Knox Press, 1996.

Middle Ages and Reformation Periods

Aquinas, Thomas, *Thomas Aquinas: Selected Writings*, Edited by Ralph McInerny. New York: Penguin Classics, 1999.

Irvin, Dale, and Scott Sunquist, *History of the World Christian Movement Volume II*. Maryknoll: Orbis Books, 2012.

Madden, Thomas, *The Concise History of the Crusades*. Lanham: Rowman and Littlefield Publishers, 2005.

Christianity in America

Applegate, Debby, *The Most Famous Man in America*. New York: Doubleday, 2006.

Butler, John, Grant Wacker, and Randall Balmer, *Religion in American Life*, New York: Oxford Press, 2008.

Gonzales, Justo, *The Story of Christianity, Volume II*, New York: Harper Collins, 2010.

Hudson, Winthrop, *Religion in America, Third Edition*, New York: Charles Scribner's Sons, 1965.

Waldman, Steven, *Founding Faith*, New York: Random House, 2008.

The Restoration Movement to Modernity

Allen, C. Leonard, and Richard T. Hughes, *Discovering Our Roots*, Abilene: ACU Press, 1988.

Allen, C. Leonard, Richard T. Hughes, and Michael R. Weed, *The Worldly Church,* Abilene: ACU Press, 1988.

Doran, Adron, *Restoring New Testament Christianity*, Nashville: 21st Century Christian, 1997.

Garrett, Leroy, *The Stone-Campbell Movement*, Joplin: College Press Publishing, 1981.

Holloway, Gary, and Douglas Foster, *Renewing God's People: A Concise History of Churches of Christ*, Abilene: Abilene Christian University Press, 2006.

Humble, Bill, *The Story of Restoration*, Pensacola: Firm Foundation Publishing House, 1969.

Journeys of Faith, Editor Robert Plummer. Grand Rapids: Zondervan, 2012.

Marsden, George, *Understanding Fundamentalism and Evangelicalism*, Grand Rapids: William B. Eerdmans Publishing, 1991.

Richardson, Robert, and Carson Reed, *Principles of the Reformation*, Villa Park: New Leaf Books, 2002.

Shepherd, J. W., *The Church, The Falling Away, and The Restoration*, Nashville: Gospel Advocate Company, 1929.

Wuthnow, Robert, *After the Baby Boomers*, Princeton: Princeton University Press, 2007.

Additional Titles by the Author

J. Terry Johnson, a native of Springfield, Missouri, retired from Oklahoma Christian University in 2000, after a thirty-two-year tenure with the Oklahoma City liberal arts university. From 1974 until 1995, Johnson was president and chief executive officer; he served an additional five years as the university's chancellor. In 2000, Johnson was inducted into the Oklahoma Higher Education Hall of Fame. He currently lives in Horseshoe Bay, Texas.

Since his retirement, Johnson has authored ten books, all of which can be purchased at www.amazon.com, www.BarnesandNoble.com, or from the author at Johnson Books, P.O. Box 8106, Horseshoe Bay, TX 78657.

Jubilee: A colorful pictorial history of the first fifty years of Oklahoma Christian University (2000).

Fairways and Green Pastures: A coffee table gift book offering an inspirational walk through each hole of Ram Rock Golf Course at the Horseshoe Bay Resort (Foreword by **Byron Nelson;** 2006).

Cardinal Fever (Foreword by **Whitey Herzog;** 2009); *Kirby* (Foreword by **John Ashcroft;** 2008); *Awakenings* (Foreword by **Pat Boone;** 2010): A trilogy of memoirs about a boy growing up in the Missouri Ozarks.

Two Parts Sunshine: A combined biography and cookbook from the life of Marty Johnson, the author's wife (Foreword by **Sherri Coale;** 2010).

10 Critical Factors in Fundraising: A digest covering the essential elements of raising financial support for nonprofit organizations (Foreword by **Andrew K. Benton;** 2011).

Be of Good Cheer: A daily devotional to encourage the reader's spiritual growth (2012).

Wounded Eagle: A novel about an imaginary Major League Baseball team in San Antonio, Texas (Foreword by **Nolan Ryan;** 2013).

A Glorious Church: A brief history of the church from its apostolic roots until the present (2015).